# THE IMPORTANCE OF

# Pancho Villa

These and other titles are included in The Importance
Of biography series:

| | |
|---|---|
| Alexander the Great | Adolf Hitler |
| Muhammad Ali | Harry Houdini |
| Louis Armstrong | Thomas Jefferson |
| Clara Barton | Chief Joseph |
| Napoleon Bonaparte | Malcolm X |
| Rachel Carson | Margaret Mead |
| Charlie Chaplin | Michelangelo |
| Cesar Chavez | Wolfgang Amadeus Mozart |
| Winston Churchill | Sir Isaac Newton |
| Cleopatra | Richard M. Nixon |
| Christopher Columbus | Georgia O'Keeffe |
| Hernando Cortes | Louis Pasteur |
| Marie Curie | Pablo Picasso |
| Amelia Earhart | Jackie Robinson |
| Thomas Edison | Anwar Sadat |
| Albert Einstein | Margaret Sanger |
| Duke Ellington | Oskar Schindler |
| Dian Fossey | John Steinbeck |
| Benjamin Franklin | Jim Thorpe |
| Galileo Galilei | Mark Twain |
| Martha Graham | Pancho Villa |
| Stephen Hawking | H. G. Wells |
| Jim Henson | |

# THE IMPORTANCE OF

# Pancho Villa

by
Bob Carroll

Lucent Books, P.O. Box 289011, San Diego, CA 92198-9011

Library of Congress Cataloging-in-Publication Data

Carroll, Bob, 1936–
    The Importance of Pancho Villa / by Bob Carroll
        p. cm.—(The Importance of)
    Includes bibliographical references (p.    ) and index.
    ISBN 1-56006-069-7
    1. Villa, Pancho, 1878–1923—Juvenile literature. 2. Mex-
ico–History—1910–1946—Juvenile literature. 3. Revolutionaries–Mexico—Biography—Juvenile literature. [1. Villa, Pancho,
1878–1923. 2. Revolutionaries. 3. Mexico—History—
1910–1946.]
    I.Title. II. Series.
F1234.V63C36      1996
972.08—dc20                                        95-11707
                                                        CIP
                                                         AC

Copyright 1996 by Lucent Books, Inc., P.O. Box 289011,
San Diego, California, 92198-9011

Printed in the U.S.A.

# Contents

# Foreword

THE IMPORTANCE OF biography series deals with individuals who have made a unique contribution to history. The editors of the series have deliberately chosen to cast a wide net and include people from all fields of endeavor. Individuals from politics, music, art, literature, philosophy, science, sports, and religion are all represented. In addition, the editors did not restrict the series to individuals whose accomplishments have helped change the course of history. Of necessity, this criterion would have eliminated many whose contribution was great, though limited. Charles Darwin, for example, was responsible for radically altering the scientific view of the natural history of the world. His achievements continue to impact the study of science today. Others, such as Chief Joseph of the Nez Percé, played a pivotal role in the history of their own people. While Joseph's influence does not extend much beyond the Nez Percé, his nonviolent resistance to white expansion and his continuing role in protecting his tribe and his homeland remain an inspiration to all.

These biographies are more than factual chronicles. Each volume attempts to emphasize an individual's contributions both in his or her own time and for posterity. For example, the voyages of Christopher Columbus opened the way to European colonization of the New World. Unquestionably, his encounter with the New World brought monumental changes to both Europe and the Americas in his day. Today, however, the broader impact of Columbus's voyages is being critically scrutinized. *Christopher Columbus,* as well as every biography in The Importance Of series, includes and evaluates the most recent scholarship available on each subject.

Each author includes a wide variety of primary and secondary source quotations to document and substantiate his or her work. All quotes are footnoted to show readers exactly how and where biographers derive their information, as well as to provide stepping stones to further research. These quotations enliven the text by giving readers eyewitness views of the life and times of each individual covered in The Importance Of series.

Finally, each volume is enhanced by photographs, bibliographies, chronologies, and comprehensive indexes. For both the casual reader and the student engaged in research, The Importance Of biographies will be a fascinating adventure into the lives of people who have helped shape humanity's past and present, and who will continue to shape its future.

# IMPORTANT DATES IN THE LIFE OF PANCHO VILLA

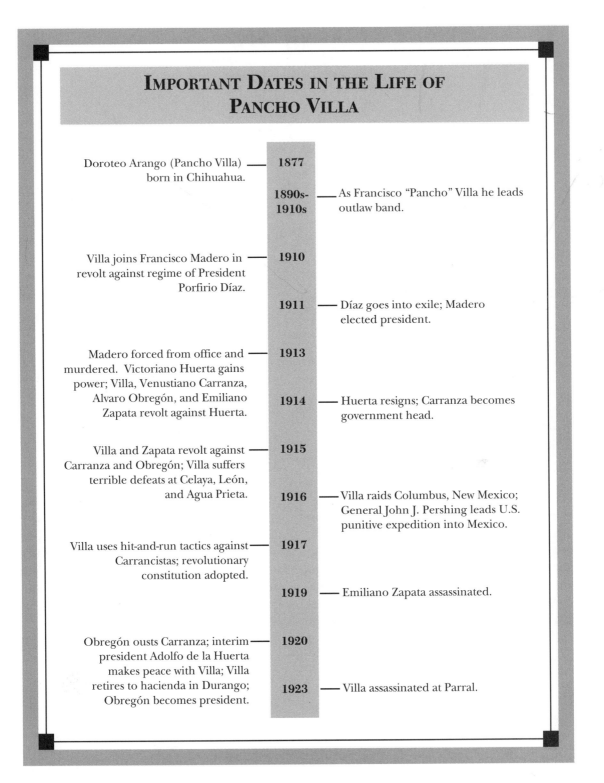

Doroteo Arango (Pancho Villa) born in Chihuahua. — **1877**

**1890s-1910s** — As Francisco "Pancho" Villa he leads outlaw band.

Villa joins Francisco Madero in revolt against regime of President Porfirio Díaz. — **1910**

**1911** — Díaz goes into exile; Madero elected president.

Madero forced from office and murdered. Victoriano Huerta gains power; Villa, Venustiano Carranza, Alvaro Obregón, and Emiliano Zapata revolt against Huerta. — **1913**

**1914** — Huerta resigns; Carranza becomes government head.

Villa and Zapata revolt against Carranza and Obregón; Villa suffers terrible defeats at Celaya, León, and Agua Prieta. — **1915**

**1916** — Villa raids Columbus, New Mexico; General John J. Pershing leads U.S. punitive expedition into Mexico.

Villa uses hit-and-run tactics against Carrancistas; revolutionary constitution adopted. — **1917**

**1919** — Emiliano Zapata assassinated.

Obregón ousts Carranza; interim president Adolfo de la Huerta makes peace with Villa; Villa retires to hacienda in Durango; Obregón becomes president. — **1920**

**1923** — Villa assassinated at Parral.

# Unusual Times, Unusual Man

American Civil War general William Sherman said, "War is hell," and few who have experienced its horrors have found reason to disagree. But if war in any form is hell, what can be said for that particularly virulent strain called revolution? Surely of all wars, that in which brother is set against brother and father against son is the most barbaric. Hatred holds sway. Honor and chivalry, rare in any war, disappear altogether. Unspeakable cruelties multiply and become the norm in revolutions, as though finding one's foe to be so much like oneself unleashes a supremely destructive primal force. All war is hell, but revolution is hell to the tenth power.

The history of Mexico for the past two hundred years is filled with revolutions; some major revolutions convulsed the entire country, some were so minor as to go unnoticed except in their particular corner of the world. But the great revolution, or series of revolutions, took place between the years 1910 and 1920. It was during this bloody time that the nation of Mexico was dragged into modernity.

The chaos of revolution often brings to the fore individuals who might otherwise merit no more than a footnote in history. They thrive amid the brutality and carnage. Such an individual was Pancho Villa, who, in the second decade of the

twentieth century, when indiscriminate bloodshed all but destroyed Mexico, rose from being an obscure outlaw to becoming a legendary military leader, a national hero, and even an international figure of some note. Of all the heroes and villains who shaped the times for Mexico, Pancho

*Pancho Villa rose from humble beginnings as an unknown outlaw to become a national hero and a symbol of Mexican pride.*

Villa's name remains the most recognizable. It is safe to say that, had there been no Pancho Villa, there still would have been a revolution in Mexico. But had there been no Mexican revolution, few outside his corner of the country would have heard of Pancho Villa.

## A Complex Personality

Although much has been written about Villa, most of it is slanted toward one aspect of his personality or another. Various personal reminiscences paint widely divergent pictures of the man—a hero, a villain, a loyal friend, a crafty deceiver, sometimes compassionate, often brutal. To tell his story one must recount the twists and turns of the Mexican revolution, including many events to which he was only an observer, because Villa's actions can only be understood and justified within the revolution's maze of changing loyalties, vaulting personal ambitions, and occasional true patriotism.

Even within the unnatural framework of revolution, Villa's was an unusual and complex personality. All agree he was totally unpredictable and subject to the most sudden and violent mood swings. Yet, because he was driven by his emotions rather than his intellect, he was often more reliable than the devious schemers he opposed. His actions, sometimes inexplicable and even self-destructive, become more understandable in retrospect if one recognizes in him an almost childlike rage to punish those he felt had harmed him. A more calculating mind might weigh the cost of vengeance and put off its execution to a later, more comfortable date.

Villa acted immediately. In effect, he shot first and asked questions later. That was his consistency.

An exceptional horseman and unerring marksman, Villa was brave to the point of being foolhardy. But it was his willingness to take risks and to inspire his soldiers to do likewise that brought him success. He was a master in the use of guerrilla, or hit-and-run, tactics, but in the strategy for larger battles, he was overtaken by time and technology. When, while the revolution still raged, the road to victory changed from bravura, all-out cavalry charges, to favor, instead, those entrenched behind machine guns and barbed wire, that same impulsive attitude that had been Villa's strength brought him his most disastrous defeats.

He prized loyalty and rewarded it. He counted among his supporters some of the most amoral cutthroats Mexico has ever known. He gave them high rank as long as they remained loyal to him, but any behavior among his followers that he deemed traitorous was certain to result in death for the scoundrel. Indeed, the incident that brought him the most notoriety—his raid on the American town of Columbus, New Mexico—was his answer to a perceived betrayal by the United States. Yet, in his personal life he placed less value on such loyalty. At his death he had four recognized widows and a fifth, until then unknown, appeared at his funeral.

Villa was uneducated and at best only semiliterate, but some of his pronouncements, though grandiose, have the ring of epic poetry. Certainly he was far from stupid. Those opponents who underestimated his intelligence usually did so to their regret.

He could be monstrously cruel to his

*Villa (center) surrounded by members of his loyal army. While Villa helped bring about much-needed changes in Mexico, his cruel and brutal tactics cannot be overlooked.*

enemies. Reports of his mass executions of prisoners filtered back to the United States and shocked even his supporters. But sadistic behavior was common to all in a war that was fought as much with terror as with weapons. What is more surprising is that Villa could be occasionally forgiving and even kind.

He began as a bandit, and to the end he remained one. Although he was more than willing to fill his own pockets with gold while conducting his revolution, he was at bottom a patriot. If he lacked any clear or consistent plan for his country except a vague wish to make things better, he nevertheless was willing to lay his life on the line for those who he believed could in the long run bring freedom, education, and prosperity to the dusty lands he warred upon. In spite of all the wanton destruction he perpetrated, he instilled a long-suppressed pride and sense of purpose in the people of his native land. And in doing so Pancho Villa, the destroyer, became also one of the builders of modern Mexico.

# 1 "Viva Villa! Viva México!"

Private Fred A. Griffin drew sentry duty on the night of March 9, 1916. He was detailed to keep watch over the encampment of less than two hundred Thirteenth U.S. Cavalry troopers stationed three miles above the Mexican border at Columbus, New Mexico. In addition to the soldiers, Columbus had a population of about a thousand people, evenly split between Americans and Mexicans. A dreary nowhere in the New Mexico desert, Columbus was described by one observer as

afflicted with windstorms and rattlesnakes; neither electricity nor telephone service had reached it . . . and its only communications with the outside world were the telegraph and the

*A triple execution at Juárez, Mexico, about the time of the Columbus raid. Rebel soldiers were notorious for their brutality, especially toward Americans.*

El Paso and Southwestern Railroad, from whose westbound "Drunkard's Special" every midnight tumbled men who had been celebrating brief furloughs [time off] in El Paso.[1]

Private Griffin, who had enlisted in the army out of Cottondale, Alabama, a year and a half earlier, had special reason to keep his eyes peeled that night. Rumor held that Pancho Villa and his army were operating somewhere nearby on the Mexican side of the border. During the time Griffin had been a soldier, 170 U.S. citizens had died at the hands of Mexicans, and most of those deaths were blamed on Villa. The most notorious incident had come in January when a group of Villistas—followers of Villa—stopped a train near Chihuahua, Mexico. The passengers—seventeen American employees of a U.S. mining company—were ordered off the train, shot, and stripped naked. Although Villa himself was not present, there was no question among Americans that the gunmen were acting under his orders.

The latest outrage had occurred nine days earlier when Villistas kidnapped a ranching family near Ciudad Juárez, Mexico, across the Rio Grande from El Paso, Texas. The rancher, John Wright, and one of his ranch hands, Frank Hayden, had been executed. Mrs. Wright was told her baby had been given to a Mexican family, and when she protested, one of Villa's men drew his sword and forced her back. Heartbroken, she was kept prisoner and forced to accompany Villa's army as it moved north.

The deaths, kidnappings, and mistreatment of Americans in Mexico caused the Cincinnati *Enquirer* to thunder: "If it takes the bayonets of our infantry, the can-

*The government of Venustiano Carranza (pictured) failed to stop the murder, kidnapping, and torture of U.S. citizens in Mexico.*

non of our artillery, the guns of our Navy, to make our citizens safe in Mexico, it must be done."[2] But most of the American press, indeed most Americans, agreed with the St. Louis *Post-Dispatch*: "This is no time to tie up the American Army and Navy."[3] Certainly not with a war raging in Europe that every day threatened to draw the United States into its morass. The San Francisco *Star* passed the buck for punishing Villa to Mexico's government, which was headed by Venustiano Carranza: "That is Carranza's job, and no American has any right to go into Mexico for that purpose without the consent of the Carranza government."[4]

For six years former bandit Pancho Villa had been one of the leading actors in Mexico's ongoing, bloody, and brutal revolution. Because in his bandit days he had often shared his plunder with the poor, he was considered a Robin Hood figure by thousands of Mexicans, particularly those in the northern states of Sonora and Chihuahua where he held sway. On the American side of the border, he was less highly regarded. Nevertheless, until the previous year or so Villa had scrupulously protected American lives and property. He had treated the United States with friendliness and honor; in turn, he had been praised by several U.S. officials.

But all that had changed suddenly. Clearly, Villa was now conducting a vendetta, or feud, against the United States. He threatened to kill any American found in Mexico. Few Americans who did not live along the border bothered to ask why. They had neither interest in nor understanding of Mexican politics. To them the simplest explanation was that, after years of opposing whichever government ruled in Mexico City, Villa had gone mad and like a wounded snake was now striking at any target that presented itself. If some foolish Americans insisted on going into Mexico, well, that was *their* problem.

Six troops of the Thirteenth U.S. Cavalry—six hundred men—had been dispatched to Columbus, New Mexico, to guard that part of the border. Their commander, Colonel Herbert J. Slocum, stationed about two hundred men in Columbus and sent the rest to Bailey's and Gibson's ranches, three and fourteen miles to the west, respectively. On March 7 Slocum received word that Villa and a large force were only two miles south of the border. But even should the report prove true, it seemed inconceivable that Villa would actually cross the border and attack, as some had predicted. That he would murder Americans within Mexico was one thing; that he would risk war by attacking the United States itself was quite different. Furthermore, at the same time the colonel received a counterreport that Villa and his men had turned south. When some of Slocum's officers asked to go to El Paso to play polo, they were granted permission.

*American troops stationed outside of Columbus, New Mexico, prepare for an attack by Villa should the wily general lead his army across the U.S. border.*

## A Bloody Escape

*Among the harrowing tales of narrow escapes during the raid, this one is repeated by Clarence C. Clendenen in* Blood on the Border.

"Lieutenant William A. McCain lived, with his wife and young daughter, in a house just south of the railroad track. That night his orderly happened to be staying at the house also. When the firing started, all four dashed out of the house and hid in the chaparral. They were joined, a few minutes later, by Captain George Williams. Williams had a pistol, and McCain and the orderly had a pistol and a shotgun. They were discovered a few minutes later by a Mexican straggler, but before he could give the alarm, McCain shot him with the shotgun, but since it was loaded with birdshot, he was not killed. The three men pulled him under a bush and choked off his cries. They were afraid to fire another shot for fear of attracting attention. One of the Americans tried to cut the man's throat with a pocket knife, but it was too dull; they finally bashed in his head with the butt of a pistol."

Nonetheless, Slocum's small company stayed alert to any possible action by the unpredictable Villa. That was why Private Griffin found himself standing watch with a rifle in the wee hours of the morning.

It was nearly 4:30 A.M. when Griffin noticed something suspicious in a long drainage ditch that ran parallel to the soldiers' encampment. He saw some movement there. When he looked closer, Griffin was able to discern a number of Mexicans moving along the ditch in preparation for attack. Villistas! Private Griffin opened fire immediately. An answering volley came from the ditch, mortally, or fatally, wounding Griffin in the stomach.

Lieutenant John P. Castleman, the officer of the day, was alone, reading in the small building that served as a sentry post. When he heard the first shots and Griffin's cry of "My God, I'm shot!" Castleman drew his revolver and rushed to the door. He was confronted by a Villista, rifle at the ready, an X of glittering bandoleers, or ammunition belts, across his chest. The Mexican fired at Castleman at point blank range—and missed! Castleman shot the man dead.

Although surprised out of their sleep, the American soldiers poured out of their quarters and returned fire. Many were only partially dressed or simply in their underwear. Rifles had been locked up for the night, with the keys now in the possession of officers. When some of the officers could not be found immediately, the locks were smashed. Others improvised weapons: one soldier killed an invader with a baseball bat, and some cooks drove off Villistas with a combination of butcher knives and boiling water. Castleman and Lieutenant John Lucas, who was to distinguish himself twenty-eight years later at the Battle of Anzio in World War II, began organizing the defense of the town.

As Villistas leaped from the ditch firing at the soldiers, mounted Mexicans rode their horses wildly through the streets of Columbus shooting at windows. "Viva Villa!" they yelled. "Viva México! Muerte a los americanos!" ("Long live Villa! Long live Mexico! Death to Americans!") They concentrated their attack on the bank, the Mercantile Store, and the Commercial Hotel. Obviously their object in the first two targets was to get supplies and money to purchase more armaments. The Villistas' interest in the Commercial Hotel was believed to stem from a deal in which owner Sam Ravel had allegedly taken money from Villa and then failed to deliver the supplies he had promised. Fortunately for Mr. Ravel, he was at that moment in El Paso undergoing treatment for sinus trouble.

One of Ravel's brothers escaped detection by hiding under a pile of hides in the Mercantile Store, but Arthur, his fifteen-year-old brother, was rousted from his bed. The Mexicans demanded the combination to the store safe. When Arthur told them he did not know the combination, they vainly attempted to open the safe by firing at it with their rifles.

According to Columbus historian Richard Dean, the first civilian casualty was Charles DeWitt Miller of Albuquerque, a guest at the Commercial Hotel: "As soon as the firing started and all the hotel guests got up, Mr. Miller started out the door and got about twenty or thirty yards outside the door and was shot dead on the spot."[5]

Suddenly fire broke out. According to most American witnesses the Villistas deliberately set fire to some buildings. Other reports indicate that the fires were accidentally started when stray bullets ignited two drums of gasoline stored across the street from the hotel. Mingled with the bloodthirsty yells, the chatter of small arms, the pounding of hooves, and the crackling of flames were the screams and cries of women and babies. As the flames grew, the last moments of night turned to day.

Ironically, the fires provided Lieutenant Castleman and a group of about twenty-five riflemen, who had advanced into the town, ample light to see their tar-

*Colonel Herbert J. Slocum (left) was doubtful that Villa would risk provoking war with the United States by crossing the U.S. border.*

*Colonel Slocum (bending over, left) consults with his staff. Slocum survived the fray in Columbus, but had a close call when his revolver was shot out of his hand by a Villista sharpshooter.*

gets. They began laying down a murderous fire. It would have been devastating had not the machine guns they set up immediately jammed.

Clad only in his underwear, young Arthur Ravel was marched down the street. Two Villista guards flanked him, apparently taking him to his execution. Army sharpshooters picked off both Villistas. Arthur began to run and did not stop until he was a mile away from the fighting.

Colonel Slocum's quarters were in the town. Awakened by the shots, he was soon in the street rushing into the fray, or battle. He reached the corner of the Hoover Hotel when, as in a scene from a Western movie, his revolver was shot out of his hand.

Columbus grocer James S. Dean was hiding in a doorway when a Villista called to him, offering him safe-conduct out of the line of fire. Dean took a few hesitant steps into the street, a shot rang out, and he fell dead.

"Viva Villa! Viva México! Muerte a los americanos!"

At the customs house A. L. Riggs, the customs officer, his wife, and three small children, barricaded themselves beneath mattresses. To prevent the baby from crying and betraying their presence to the Villistas, Mrs. Riggs stuffed a pillowcase in the child's mouth. The station agent for the El Paso and Southwestern Railroad and his family hid on the second floor of the railroad station. In the nearby station house foreman S. H. McCullough and his wife huddled on the floor with their four children as bullets whizzed over their heads.

The Villistas discovered A. L. Ritchie, the proprietor, when they entered the Commercial Hotel. Upstairs they found Walton Walker, a delegate to the New Mexico Convention of Sunday Schools, and his wife Rachel. One Mexican told Walker he wanted him to come downstairs and shake hands with his captain. "And they took Walker down the steps," Jessie Thompson, a descendant of a survivor, recounts. "His little bride clung to him and they threw her aside. My grandmother said he made a motion to help her and they shot him on the steps."[6] Downstairs, Ritchie begged for his life. He emptied his pockets and produced fifty dollars. The Villistas took the money and then killed him.

Meanwhile, the hotel was becoming engulfed in flames. Two U.S. customs border guards, Jolly Garner and Ben Aguirre, tied sheets to Mrs. Walker's arms and lowered her to safety from an upstairs window before escaping themselves.

Many of the army officers quartered in town with their families were unable to join the other soldiers because of the swarming Villistas. As best they could, they fortified their homes and protected their wives and children. Some wives were alone, their officer husbands on duty elsewhere. Such was the case of Mrs. Thomas Ryan whose husband was on border patrol. She decided her adobe garage was more bullet proof than her small house. As she ran from the building, a Villista appeared and grabbed her by the arm. "Where are you going?" he demanded in Spanish.

"Nowhere," shouted Mrs. Ryan. The Villista nodded and released her.[7]

The battle continued until nearly 6:30 A.M., when dawn came. Along with it the soldiers from Bailey's ranch arrived to reinforce the troopers in Columbus. Bugles sounded, ordering Villa's men to withdraw. On their way they stopped to loot the ranch of J. J. Moore. The rancher was taken out of his house and murdered on his doorstep. Mrs. Moore was wounded in the thigh. She and Mrs. John Wright, the woman who had been held captive by Villa for nine days, were discovered in a field by American soldiers.

*American troops pursue the retreating Villistas into Mexico. Greatly outnumbered and nearly out of ammunition, the American troops were forced to withdraw from the pursuit.*

*Columbus, New Mexico, after Villa's raid. The raid left the town, and many Americans, seething with animosity toward Villa and Mexico.*

Major Frank Tomkins found Colonel Slocum and obtained permission to organize a pursuit of the retreating Villistas. Tomkins took Troop H and followed the Mexicans. Later he was joined by Lieutenant Castleman and 27 men from Troop F, bringing his force to about 220. The pursuing band was far smaller than Villa's force, but the Mexicans apparently did not realize just how few were the gnats at their heels. In a series of firefights, or gun battles, Tomkins and his men followed the Villistas fifteen miles into Mexico. One American corporal was reported killed in the fighting. Eventually Tomkins forged ahead with a tiny force of 35 men. At last the Mexicans became aware that they vastly outnumbered the American force; they turned and charged. By then, Tomkins's men were nearly out of ammunition. However, they were able to withdraw in good order without losing a man. Tomkins admitted, "I received a slight wound in the knee, a bullet through the rim of my hat and my horse was wounded slightly in the head."[8] He was awarded the Distinguished Service Cross for bravery. His troopers enthusiastically claimed to have killed one hundred Mexicans in the pursuit, but battle estimates of the times were normally absurdly inflated and could often be divided by ten.

Villa's booty from the raid included a great deal of military equipment, including three hundred Mauser repeating rifles, but much of it was abandoned in the retreat to Mexico. The Villistas also stole eighty horses and thirty mules—about the same number as they lost in the raid. Twenty-seven Villista bodies were counted in Columbus. For sanitary purposes they were gathered together and burned, then buried in a mass grave.

Anti-Mexican feeling ran high in Columbus. One wounded Mexican prisoner lay on the ground. When a rancher strode by, the Mexican begged for a drink. "I'll give you a drink," snarled the rancher. He drew his pistol and shot the wounded man. The authorities never considered prosecuting the rancher.[9]

American losses were actually quite small. Nine civilians and eight troopers died; eight people, including six soldiers, were wounded. Part of the reason for the

light losses was the uniformly poor marksmanship of the Villistas, but the main reason was that, despite hysterical American
claims, the raid was not designed to kill innocent civilians or even U.S. soldiers. Ad-
mittedly a few Villistas engaged in
cold-blooded murder, but the purpose of
the raid was to gain supplies—guns, ammunition, horses, food, and money—so
that Villa could continue fighting his revolution in Mexico.

That and to tweak Uncle Sam's nose.

## America Reacts

If Pancho Villa wanted to get the United
States' attention with his raid on Columbus, he could not have succeeded more
completely. By the next day his name was
in headlines in every American newspaper. Americans who only a few days before
had barely known who Villa was or who
had not recognized his name at all, now
read long, sometimes fictionalized, accounts of his life and exploits in newspapers and magazines.

Only the most naive believed that
Villa's army intended a full-scale invasion
of the United States, but stories made the
rounds that he was actually being financed
by Germany as a way of keeping America
occupied on its own border and out of the
war in Europe. No less than James Gerard,
the U.S. ambassador in Berlin, telegraphed
home, "Am sure Villa's attacks are made
[originate] in Germany." In April, *Collier's
Magazine*, a respected journal of the day,
laid the blame at Germany's door.

The truth, of course, was that Villa was
not being financed by anyone. His short-
age of equipment and the wherewithal to

buy it was why he felt he was forced to
make his raid. Furthermore, to imagine
the nationalistic Villa putting his men and
cause at risk at the will of some European
puppeteers strains credibility. If in his career Villa did not always act wisely, he always acted for Villa and Mexico.

Most Americans settled for a simple
explanation: Villa was a bloodthirsty bandit acting like a bloodthirsty bandit. To
hell with what made him tick—he must be
punished! In the wake of the Columbus
raid, few were the voices raised against intervention.

The *New York Times* boomed: "Villa
must be suppressed. His villainous activities must be stopped for all time, and we
must do it."[10]

Venustiano Carranza, recognized by
Washington as the legitimate head of Mexico's government, immediately apologized
and promised "the most vigorous means"
to hunt down Villa. That was not good
enough for America. The day after the
raid President Woodrow Wilson declared
that the United States would send an
armed punitive, or punishing, force into
Mexico.

The *New York Times* editorialized:

In announcing that a force of American troops will be sent across the border without delay, with the single
object of capturing Villa, the President
informs the country that this action
will be taken "in entirely friendly aid
of the constituted [established] authorities in Mexico and with scrupu-
lous respect for the sovereignty of that
republic." We know that he means exactly what he says, and we know that
the dispatch of troops into Mexico at
this time for the designated purpose

## Blame?

*This passage from Clarence C. Clendenen's* Blood on the Border *suggests that Americans could be just as hysterical in searching for someone to blame in 1916 as they sometimes are today.*

"Extreme pacifists and certain professional liberals immediately charged that the whole affair [raid on Columbus] was a fake. Villa, some said, was not really responsible. The real responsibility rested on the bankers and industrialists of 'Wall Street,' who callously plotted the murder of American citizens and soldiers in order to force intervention and thereby safeguard their Mexican investments. That most officers and many soldiers lived outside the camp came in for a great deal of ignorant criticism—criticism that ignored that no quarters for married people were provided at Columbus. Lieutenant Lucas was criticized because his machine guns . . . jammed repeatedly during the action. The objection . . . ignores the obvious: That Lieutenant Lucas had nothing to do with the design or adoption of the weapon. . . . There was a loud demand for a scapegoat, and Colonel Herbert Slocum was a natural target. It was quickly shown, however, that he had taken every precaution that was possible."

cannot fairly be construed to mean armed intervention. It is a purely punitive expedition, and it is undertaken only because the Carranza Government is obviously unable to preserve order.[11]

The *Times* went on to explain that "any intelligent Mexican" would agree with all this.

In other words, the United States was joyfully launching a "friendly" invasion of a neighboring country. Mexican citizens were expected to welcome these armed invaders of their country with open arms because, after all, the foreigners were only there to capture or kill a Mexican hero and anyone who supported him. The United States took this friendly action because Mexicans had proved incapable of running their own affairs. And any Mexican who did not see things from the American point of view was just too stupid to count anyway.

Such tortured logic would not wash in Chihuahua. Regardless of how Villa was viewed north of the border, his stock skyrocketed in Mexico.

# 2 Heritage of Blood

Pancho Villa's critics often focus on his violence and his undeniable acts of cruelty. But in truth, long before Villa rode across the Mesa del Norte (Northern Plateau), Mexico's history was steeped in blood. Villa's career is simply a continuation of the turmoil that racked, or afflicted, Mexico from its beginnings.

During the time that Rome rose and fell, great Indian civilizations flourished in Mexico, leaving behind huge stone pyramids dedicated to the sun and the moon. Some of these still stand today at Teotihuacán near Mexico City. The last and greatest of the Indian civilizations was that of the Aztecs who created an ocean-to-ocean empire in the mid-1400s. Their capital, Tenochtitlán, stood on an island in Lake Texcoco, the present site of Mexico City. It contained over 100,000 people, making it larger than any city in Spain at the time. Like the civilizations before them, the Aztecs performed human sacrifice and enslaved other tribes.

In 1519 tales of gold, silver, and precious gems brought the Spanish conqueror Hernando Cortés to the shores of Mexico with a force of six hundred men. Although greatly outnumbered by the Aztecs, Cortés quickly found allies among other native tribes who had long suffered under the Aztec yoke. However, Cortés's greatest weapon was the wonder caused by his horses, cannon, and armor. The Indians, who had never seen such things, thought the Spaniards must be gods.

Montezuma II, the Aztec emperor, sent rich gifts to Cortés, hoping they would satisfy him and he would then

*A remnant of Mexico's colorful past, the impressive pyramids of Teotihuacán are a reminder of the great Indian civilizations that once flourished there.*

*Sixteenth-century Aztec emperor Montezuma was a powerful ruler whose influence extended far beyond the boundaries of his mighty empire.*

country was ruled from Spain. Mexico was far larger at the time, encompassing much of what is now the United States, including Texas, New Mexico, Arizona, California, and large parts of other American states. Much of the land was divided into huge haciendas, or ranches, owned by Creoles (people of European descent born in Mexico) and mestizos (people of mixed European and Indian ancestry). Both the Creoles and mestizos considered themselves superior to the native Indians. While the hacienda owners grew rich, the Indians who worked on the haciendas remained in poverty.

The first stirrings of revolution came in the early 1800s. During the next hundred years revolution would be a constant in Mexican history—revolution and war-

*Believing that the Spaniards were gods, Montezuma allowed Cortés to enter Tenochtitlán. Their historic meeting is depicted here.*

leave. Instead, the bribes only whetted his appetite for more. Still afraid that the invaders might be gods, Montezuma foolishly allowed Cortés to enter Tenochtitlán. Cortés's tiny army could never control the vast Aztec empire, but he soon made Montezuma his prisoner and ruled through him. The Aztecs revolted in 1520, killed Montezuma, and drove Cortés out of the city. Only the intervention of friendly tribes of Indians who fought beside the Spanish saved his expedition from annihilation. Six months later he returned with another Spanish force and a large army of Indians and laid siege to Tenochtitlán. In August of 1521 Cuauhtémoc, the last Aztec emperor, surrendered. Spain controlled Mexico.

For nearly three hundred years the

fare with Mexico's northern neighbor. Pancho Villa was hardly a student of history, but he was its product. Events that took place long before he was born shaped the Mexico he lived in and his reaction to it.

## An Independent Nation

Mexico's first revolutionary leaders were Catholic priests. In 1810 Miguel Hidalgo y Costilla called for separation from Spain. Although he had some initial success, he was opposed by most of the Creoles who wished only for a relaxation of some Spanish control. In 1811 Hidalgo was captured and executed by Spanish troops. His fight was taken up by another priest, José Maria Morales y Pavon, who advanced the cause for independence by writing a constitution for a proposed Mexican republic. But Morales was also captured and executed in 1815, and most of his followers were killed or imprisoned.

The movement toward independence might have ended there had it not been for a mistake made by the Spanish king, Ferdinand VII. He decided that all Mexicans were traitors and imposed harsh taxes and laws that drove the previously loyal Creoles to the side of revolution. In 1820, while Ferdinand was weakened by an uprising at home, the leader of the Spanish army in Mexico joined forces with the main revolutionary leader. Within a year Mexico had become an independent country.

Although at last independent, Mexican leaders were deeply divided between those who wanted a monarchy with an emperor and those who wanted a republic with a president. Additionally, some favored a strong central government while others wanted the bulk of power to rest with the various Mexican states. A third bone of contention was whether to install Roman Catholicism as the national religion or to establish freedom of religion for all. There were frequent uprisings as one faction or another attempted to take power.

In 1833 a military man, General Antonio López de Santa Anna, became president and a year later made himself

---

### Santa Anna: No Saint

*In* Hello Mexico *Morris Weeks Jr. describes General Antonio López de Santa Anna.*

"Santa Anna was short, fat-stomached, bulb-nosed, and immensely conceited. He fancied himself as an administrator and as a military strategist. In the first capacity he repeatedly raided the slender national treasury, then borrowed from foreign bankers and squandered the proceeds."

*Antonio López de Santa Anna, a military man, ruled Mexico as president eleven times between 1833 and 1855.*

dictator. By far the most important and most able Mexican leader of the time, Santa Anna, a mestizo, held power for most of the next quarter century. He was either elected to or captured the office of president eleven different times. But each time he was overthrown. His greatest failing would seem to be that he had no real program for Mexico except his own achievement of power. When he died in 1876, he was impoverished.

## The Northern Neighbor

During this time more and more Americans had moved into northern Mexico, an area that is now Texas, where they established ranches and other businesses. Generally, they behaved independently of the government in Mexico City. When Santa

Anna tried to change the constitution to give himself more control over the provinces, the Texans revolted. The most famous incident of the Texans' war for independence was the Battle of the Alamo at San Antonio in 1836, where fewer than two hundred Texans under the command of Colonel William Travis barricaded themselves in the local mission and held off Santa Anna and an army of four thousand for thirteen days. Among the defenders were the famous American frontiersmen Davey Crockett and Jim Bowie. At last Santa Anna was able to storm the Alamo; none of the Texans survived.

However, by delaying Santa Anna, the defenders of the Alamo were able to give General Sam Houston time to gather his forces. A month and a half later at the Battle of San Jacinto, with the rallying cry "Remember the Alamo!" Houston defeated the Mexican army, captured Santa Anna, and forced him to sign a treaty granting independence to Texas. The newly independent territory was nearly a quarter the size of Mexico and also included parts of present-day Colorado, Kansas, New Mexico, Oklahoma, and Wyoming.

The treaty had, of course, been signed under duress, or force, and the Mexican government did not recognize it as valid. Clashes along the Texas-Mexico border were common. In 1845 the United States annexed Texas, and the following year, when U.S. and Mexican troops fought along the border, the United States declared war on Mexico, announcing that Mexico had invaded U.S. territory even though all the fighting had taken place on land claimed by both nations. In fact, the United States had been attempting to purchase California, New Mexico, and the dis-

*The Texans' war for independence from Mexico culminated in the Battle of the Alamo. During this thirteen-day battle, fewer than two hundred barricaded Texans bravely held off a Mexican army of four thousand.*

puted Texas areas from Mexico, but was stymied by the unwillingness of Mexican leaders to appear weak in making concessions to the United States. War with Mexico was a convenient way for the United States to acquire the Mexican lands it desired.

While one U.S. army pushed into Mexico from the north, another ten thousand troops under General Winfield Scott landed in Veracruz in March 1847. Although the Mexican army was superior in numbers, it was poorly equipped and badly led. By September Scott's army was in Mexico City. Part of his force was made up of U.S. Marines; their entry into the Mexican capital is commemorated in the Marine hymn in the opening line: "From the halls of Montezuma."

On February 2, 1848, Mexico ceded 525,000 square miles of territory to the United States. For what was to become the states of California, Nevada, Utah, most of Arizona, and parts of New Mexico, Colorado, and Wyoming, the United States paid the trifling sum of fifteen million dollars. Five years later the United States acquired the remainder of the modern states of Arizona and New Mexico in another purchase.

# Benito Juárez

Mexico was devastated by its war with the United States, and the war allowed Santa Anna to seize power as dictator once more in 1853. However, a liberal movement under the leadership of Benito Juárez, a Zapotec Indian from the state of Oaxaca, drove Santa Anna out of office two years later and began to institute land reform. The liberals hoped to break up the huge haciendas, including many held by the Catholic Church, and divide the land into smaller farms. This action brought another revolution in 1858—this one by the conservative landowners, supported by the church. For a time the conservatives held power in Mexico City, but late in 1860 the liberals under Juárez regained control.

By now the Mexican government was nearly destitute, or impoverished. Juárez announced a stop to repayment of debts to France, Great Britain, and Spain. As a result, troops from all three nations occupied Veracruz in 1862. Normally this would have brought them into conflict with the United States, whose Monroe Doctrine prohibited European nations from interfering in the affairs of the Americas. However, at that moment, the United States was engaged in its own civil war and could pay little attention to happenings in Mexico.

Spain and Great Britain soon withdrew from Veracruz, but France had a different agenda. French troops invaded and captured Mexico City. With support from Mexican conservatives the French emperor placed Archduke Maximilian, a brother of the Austrian emperor, on the throne as his puppet ruler of Mexico. Juárez and the liberals were reduced to fighting a guerrilla war against the invaders. But with the end of the American Civil War, the United States put pressure on France and forced the withdrawal of its troops from Mexico in 1867. Shorn of his army, Maximilian was arrested, tried, and shot. Once more Juárez and the liberal movement were in power.

Benito Juárez was, without doubt, a great man. He sought power only to use it to improve the lot of the Mexican people, particularly the most downtrodden. Under his leadership the liberal government worked toward land reform, separation of church and state, and religious toleration. Unfortunately for Mexico, Juárez died of a heart attack in 1872. Within four years a

*A champion for the rights of the poor and downtrodden, Benito Juárez worked for land reform, separation of church and state, and religious tolerance.*

new, larger-than-life ruler sent Mexico spinning in a new direction.

## Porfirio Díaz

Like Juárez, Porfirio Díaz was born in Oaxaca, Mexico. Of mixed Indian and Spanish parentage, he studied for the priesthood and then turned to the law. He first achieved prominence as a general fighting the French forces that had placed Maximilian on the throne. In 1871 Díaz opposed Juárez for the presidency, and when his candidacy failed, he attempted unsuccessfully to lead a revolt. Defeated again, he was forced to flee north into hiding. In 1876 he unseated Juárez's successor and proclaimed himself provisional president. The following year he was elected to the office.

Díaz's first term as president was low-key. Essentially, he prepared for the future by weakening his enemies and rewarding his friends. According to an amendment to the Mexican constitution, a president could not hold the office for two successive terms. In 1880 Díaz was able to engineer the election of one of his henchmen, Manuel González, who could be counted on to retire in favor of his sponsor once his term ended. Furthermore, González was so inept and so greedy that when Díaz was ready to resume power, he looked like a godsend by comparison. González not only looted the state treasury, he even stole the furniture from the National Palace! When Díaz again became president in 1884, a grateful nation easily set aside the no reelection restriction. Díaz was back to stay.

At first Díaz was thought of as a liberal.

Even when it became clear that he was an absolute dictator, many in Mexico and nearly all international commentators believed him to be a benevolent dictator. It was many years before it became clear how few were his beneficiaries and how many were his victims.

His harshest critics had to admit that he achieved peace during his reign. The country had been torn by one revolution after another—interspersed with occasional wars against the United States—for more than sixty years when Díaz took office. Constant, wrenching changes at the top had prevented Mexico from following any long-term policies. No sooner would the nation set itself on one path than a new government would change its direc-

*Porfirio Díaz was an iron-fisted dictator who brought temporary peace to Mexico, but whose corrupt regime set the stage for the bloodiest revolution of all.*

## Juárez and Santa Anna

*In* The Men Who Made Mexico *Clarke Newlon discusses a famous meeting.*

"While [Benito] Juárez was still in school, in 1829, Santa Anna came through Oaxaca and was tendered [offered] a dinner by officials of the Institute. He recalled later with some bitterness—because the two men became mortal enemies—that waiting his table that night was a bare-footed young man in linen breeches [pants] whose name he discovered by chance to be Benito Juárez. Santa Anna always preferred to believe that it was this incident—emphasizing the difference in their stations in life—that turned Juárez against him. It probably didn't occur to him that it was his morals and not his money which Juárez despised."

tion. Moreover, the continuous fighting for leadership disrupted the economy and drenched the land in blood and hate. No doubt a spate of uninterrupted peace was Mexico's greatest need. Díaz brought peace—but at a dreadful cost. And in the long run he set the stage for the bloodiest revolution of all.

According to historian Ronald Atkin:

Díaz offered Mexicans the alternative of *pan o palo*, bread or the club. A dog with a bone in its mouth neither kills nor steals, he philosophized, offering the bone of power and prestige to all the dissatisfied elements. He bought the loyalty of some by gifts of *haciendas*, concessions or cash. If they refused the *pan*, the *palo* was wielded mercilessly. All possible instigators of opposition—landowners, clergy, army, intelligentsia [intellectuals] and even the bandit chiefs—were converted into followers of Don Porfirio. He did not amass a personal fortune but he spent millions on keeping what he wanted, the dictatorship. He gave away the country's wealth in the form of privileges, monopolies and concessions to all those who might be able to help him towards this end.[12]

One of Díaz's most successful, and most cynical, moves was to form the bandits who roved the countryside into the Guardia Rural, a twisted version of the Canadian Mounties. In effect, he seemed to stop crime in rural areas by legalizing the criminals; the *rurales*, as they were known, were licensed to steal. Heavily armed and ornately uniformed by Díaz, these so-called policemen were turned loose to prey on the poor farmers in their districts. Only Díaz's wealthy supporters and foreign investors were off-limits. Díaz let his *rurales* keep their loot. He was interested in power, and through his vicious *rurales* he kept the downtrodden in rural areas of Mexico pacified by terror, while allowing his allies to prosper and, of course, remain in his debt.

The *rurales*' brutality knew no bounds. Dissenters against government policies or landowners' wishes were tortured and killed without compunction. When a group of Hidalgo Indians resisted government confiscation of their land, the *rurales* buried them up to their necks and galloped their horses over them. To preserve an appearance of legality, prisoners were usually said to have been shot while attempting to escape. During Díaz's reign more than ten thousand prisoners were unsuccessful in "escape" attempts. Díaz bragged to foreign journalists that the Mexican countryside was safer than Hyde Park in London. It was—except for the Mexicans.

Any bandit who for conscience, pride, or personal ambition refused to join the Guardia Rural was ruthlessly hunted down and killed. Pancho Villa managed to avoid such a fate. Informers seldom betrayed him because of his practice of sharing the spoils of his bandit raids with the poor of the district. His intimate knowledge of the mountainous terrain of northwestern Mexico served him well in many narrow escapes. And he was quickly developing a sense for recognizing danger. A rancher who met Villa during those days remarked, "His eyes never missed a thing, and they never gave anything away either."[13]

Under President Díaz justice became a joke. Cases were decided not on merit but on the standing of the accused with the regime and with the size of the bribe the judge received. Those judges who refused to be bribed by Díaz's supporters were imprisoned by Díaz's soldiers. An American commented tongue-in-cheek: "Justice is really much more satisfactory in Mexico than in the United States. [In the United States] you never know how your case is coming out. [In Mexico] you know to the peso the price of each judge."[14]

Díaz found an important ally in the church. Where Juárez had sought to separate church and state and to redistribute some of the church's vast landholdings, Díaz tied the church and his government together and refused to enforce any of Juárez's land reforms. As a result, propaganda urging support for Díaz could be heard coming from most church pulpits on Sundays.

The legislature was appointed by Díaz. About a dozen seats were set aside for his relatives; the rest were handed out as rewards to Díaz loyalists. Elections were held, of course, but the winners were known before any ballots were cast. Opponents of Díaz candidates might be beaten or imprisoned. Ballot boxes were stuffed. In one state prisoners were set to marking large piles of ballots with X's next to the names of the Díaz candidates. Historian Ronald Atkin wrote:

So Díaz ruled Mexico with what was called at the time "the most perfect one-man system on earth." He appointed the governors of the twenty-seven states and gave them license to tyrannize in return for their loyalty. These men in turn appointed the *jefes politicos* [political leaders]. So the staircase of power was built: minor officials answerable to the detested *jefes*, who were in turn answerable to the governors. And they answered to their master, Díaz.[15]

Such a corrupt system took a great deal of money to run, and when Díaz came to power, years of war and revolution followed by the greedy González regime had left the treasury empty and the nation drowning in foreign debt. Díaz

*President Díaz and his cabinet hold a meeting at the National Palace. Díaz rigged elections and appointed only loyal family members and friends to government posts.*

replenished the nation's coffers by selling his country off piece by piece at bargain prices. Foreign investors were given highly advantageous terms to exploit Mexico's resources. Foreign companies, particularly American-owned corporations, controlled huge cattle ranches and enormous sugar, coffee, and maguey cactus estates. Oil was discovered on the Gulf Coast at the end of the nineteenth century, setting off a new boom of foreign investment. Money flowed out of Mexico, but at the same time the national treasury, Díaz, and his supporters were enriched by taxes, kickbacks, graft, and bribes. Naturally, foreigners who were growing rich at the expense of ordinary Mexicans lavished praise on the Díaz regime.

From the beginning Díaz realized that the one group he need not fear and, therefore, need not reward, was the great mass of ordinary people, particularly the Indians. Without leaders, without education, without political power of any kind, without hope, the majority of the population could be ignored or exploited or sacrificed for the benefit of the Díaz regime. Parcels of land owned by poor Indians since the days of Spanish rule could be easily confiscated, for even if deeds existed, their owners could not read them. Peons could be arrested and used as slave labor on the most transparent of trumped-up charges.

The stereotypical picture of the Mexican peasant that was accepted by the world and encouraged by the Díaz regime was of an ignorant, lazy, untrustworthy, drunken sot passed out during siesta against an adobe wall. The world could waste little sympathy on such worthless trash.

*Chapter*

# 3 A False Dawn

In 1877, the year after Díaz came to power, Pancho Villa was born into semi-slavery in Rio Grande, a village in the state of Durango. He was christened Doroteo Arango. Little is known of his early years, but they could not have been dissimilar from the bleak existence of other boys on the hacienda. He received no schooling; he could neither read nor write. At the age when American youngsters were starting first grade, he was put to work alongside other peon children in the fields. It was hot, dusty work from dawn to dusk. Peon children found little time for play. All young Doroteo could look forward to was a misery-filled future of backbreaking labor, dreary poverty, and, finally, death. Under such circumstances the spirits of most boys were crushed by the time they reached their teens. Yet somehow against all likelihood, in the heart of young Doroteo flamed the fire of independence.

Years later Soledad Seanez, one of his wives, recalled:

Pancho Villa was not cultivated in the art of letters but could never be called ignorant. He had almost no chance at schooling when he was a child. He and all his people had to work like slaves from daylight to dark on the hacienda where he was born. He grew up suffer-ing the cruelties and injustices of a brutal *patron* [landlord] system under a wealthy Spanish don [noble]. All his life he hated those aristocratic *patrones* [landlords].

Even more than he hated dons Villa hated the ignorance that kept the Mexican people crushed and hopeless. That's why he tried so hard to build schools and keep them going. When a powerful, ambitious, brilliant man like my husband is held down to slavery, is tied to a post and flogged when he tried to run away, hunted down and sent to rot in jail as a teenager, when his father dies from overwork, then is when hate grows. He promised himself vengeance.[16]

Doroteo learned to ride a horse and to shoot a rifle. By the time he was ten, he was among his village's best horsemen and marksmen. When he found a chance to slip away with a borrowed rifle, he usually brought back a rabbit or other small game to add to his family's meager diet. Doroteo was only thirteen when his father died. Barely a teenager, he became the man of the house. Seanez wrote:

There seemed no chance to better himself. There was hardly hope of enough tortillas and beans to keep his mother and younger brothers and sisters alive. So what does Villa do? He rebels. Very young he steals what he cannot get any other way. He becomes defiant and daring and the first chance he had he took to make money the only way he could, by stealing. His mother was very strict and honest. When Villa brought her money he stole she felt very bad. She cried and wouldn't accept it, though there was no other way for a boy like Villa to survive. He was not a thief by nature, but there was no other way to live.[17]

According to legend, one day when Doroteo was fifteen years old, he returned from the fields to find his mother greatly upset and weeping. The *hacendado* (landlord) had just raped Doroteo's younger sister. Doroteo went to the home of a peon who owned a rifle and borrowed the weapon. When he returned, he found the *hacendado* and shot him dead. Before he could be arrested, he escaped to the Sierra Madre (mountain range).

There are differing versions of this tale. In some, Doroteo is sixteen. The rapist is sometimes the *hacendado*'s son, sometimes an overseer. In some versions Doroteo arrives just as his sister is being attacked and dispatches the would-be rapist with a knife. Regardless of the details, by the time he was in his mid-teens, the young man was on the run from the law.

Living by his wits in the mountains was anything but easy. Soledad Seanez wrote:

He told me of the terrible hardships of those days. There was never any rest or peace. He suffered from dirt and lice. He had not even a handkerchief. No one knew how he suffered. Villa joined a group of men in similar circumstances. Being a natural leader, he was soon leading the bandit band.[18]

He also changed his name to Francisco Villa, the name of an outlaw from an earlier era whom he admired. However, it

As a teenager, Villa joined a group of bandits and soon became their leader. This small band of outlaws evolved into Villa's loyal company of followers known as the Villistas (pictured).

*The heavily armed Mexican* rurales *roamed the countryside, looting and terrorizing rural citizens. For more than twelve years Villa managed to thwart repeated attempts by these so-called policemen to capture him.*

was as the even more robust-sounding "*pancho*" Villa that he became known.

The term *outlaw* conjures visions of daring train and bank robberies. In truth, most of Villa's outlawry was simple cattle rustling. Occasionally he and his followers might steal a couple of dozen steers from one of the big haciendas. In such a case the bulk of the small herd would be driven north across the border and sold to American ranchers there. More often the take was only a cow or two—food for Villa and his band.

If a wagon or coach happened to stray into the outlaws' territory, it would be stopped and the riders relieved of their valuables, but such windfalls were rare. When opportunities for banditry dried up, Villa took jobs as a ranch hand under his own name, Doroteo Arango. Some-

times he worked for the same ranchers he had rustled from earlier.

For more than a dozen years the young outlaw ranged the Sierra Madre with a band of devoted followers. Many attempts were made by *rurales* and posses of ranchers to capture him, but he always managed to escape, sometimes by the narrowest of margins. His exploits soon took on a Robin Hood quality. His victims were the rich *hacendados*; the spoils of his raids were often shared with the local peons. For example, if the Villistas rustled a herd of cattle, the poorest families in the district might add some welcome beef to their diets. A few of the coins stolen in a robbery might find their way into peon hands.

Cynics could point out that it was only natural that Villa would rob the rich. The poor of the district had nothing worth stealing. And by sharing a small portion of his booty with the people, he ensured their gratitude and made it unlikely they would inform the *rurales* of his band's location or movements. No doubt there was a practical side to Villa's Robin Hood tactics, but his subsequent career makes it clear that he had a real empathy for the poor and a consuming hatred for their exploiters. He once said, "When you give to the people you are closer to heaven than at any other time in your life, for you are being directed by the Hand of God."[19]

His daredevil deeds made him a hero far more than his acts of charity did. He was brave, sometimes to the point of foolhardiness. He was a fine horseman and generally regarded as the most deadly shot in the land.

In many ways he was an enigma, or mystery. Even his most loyal lieutenants feared his sudden mood shifts. One second he could be affable and kind, the next cruel and unforgiving, and then, just as suddenly, return to pleasantness. One observer quoted by Charles Flandrau described him as

a creature of wild and contradictory impulses . . . at times he would take a malignant pleasure in human suffering . . . and then suddenly, overwhelmed by a wave of maudlin tenderness, would perform an act which, emanating from a normal individual, would be classed as magnanimous. He was a token and portent [omen] of the period, and his name the symbol under which all the delirium, the savagery, the disconcerting confusion of those troublous times were focused and epitomized.[20]

*Although notorious for his volatility and violent mood swings, Villa was admired as a brave and inspirational leader.*

Although Villa was an inspirational leader with legions of followers, he was not physically impressive. Unlike so many leaders of the time, he disdained elaborate uniforms. Of medium height, stocky to the point of chubbiness, he had short, bowed legs and walked with a pigeon-toed, shambling gait. Only on horseback did he appear heroic. His hair was brown and kinky. His face was dominated by a droopy mustache and often by a toothy smile. But his eyes were small and, according to some, glittered with the cold light of a born killer.

Though he did not have movie star

looks, women found him extremely attractive. According to Peterson and Knoles, "He was a great lover, marrying many times without the benefit of divorce, having many sweethearts, not all of whom were willing. He called himself a 'son-of-a-bitch with women,' and was acknowledged to be *muy hombre.*"[21]

For more than fifteen years, Villa followed a successful career as a bandit. But far greater things awaited him.

## The Haciendas

The longer the Díaz regime stayed in power, the more the land was concentrated in the hands of a few. Three thousand families owned almost half of the land in Mexico by 1910. The half that was left was virtually worthless—either dense jungle or dry desert. Peons who once had been able to scratch out a meager sustenance on small plots of their own were reduced to working as serfs on the great haciendas.

Each hacienda had its own *tienda de raya,* similar to what would be called the company store in some areas of the United States. The store belonged to the owner of the hacienda, and his peons were forced to make all their purchases there. In most cases peons were paid in tokens that could be used only at the *tienda de raya*; sometimes they were paid in goods. Wages were infinitesimal; a man working full-time might earn fifty cents in a week. As a result, his debt at the store was always greater than what he could earn, effectively binding him to the hacienda. Peons were born into the debts of their fathers and passed those and their

own debts on to their children. Escape was nearly impossible. Away from the hacienda lay only starvation for a person without resources or skills, unless he was willing to chance banditry.

A few—a very few—hacienda owners treated their workers humanely; most treated them as slaves. Some even put them in chains. Many *hacendados* spent little time on their vast estates, preferring the social whirl of Mexico City. The overseers left to run the haciendas could improve their own situations by getting the most work for the least cost from the peons. Beatings were the usual way of urging harder work. If a peon happened to be beaten to death, the

*Reputed to be quite popular with women, Villa married numerous times and had many lovers. He is pictured here in 1914 with one of his wives.*

overseer would never be prosecuted. Peons could always be replaced.

As many as three thousand peons might live on a hacienda, usually in huts of bamboo and thatch with dirt floors. Since separate housing was seldom provided for the hacienda's animals, peons shared their quarters with them. Some American observers wrote in admiration that the peons were allowed to live on the haciendas rent free!

According to one who studied the peons' diet, the intake of calories was barely enough to furnish the energy necessary for a person "at absolute rest." The peons' diet was almost entirely beans and corn laced with chili to make them almost di-

gestible. Most peons suffered from a variety of digestive disorders. To calm the effects of their diet and, in a sense, escape from their lives, peons drank great quantities of pulque, the fermented juice of the maguey cactus. One observer, commenting on the stereotypical view of the lazy, drunken peon, said:

> One marvels . . . not that they are dirty but that under the circumstances they are as clean as they are; not that so many of them are continually sick, but that any of them are ever well; not that they love to get drunk, but that they can bear to remain sober.[22]

One might expect people so downtrodden to be ever on the verge of revolt, but such was not the case. The *hacendados* had the law, the church, and, if necessary, the *rurales*. They had the weapons and the ruthlessness to use them. A necessity for revolution is hope. The peons had none.

## Díaz Is Opposed

At times it must have seemed that Porfirio Díaz would reign in Mexico forever. As the world entered the twentieth century, few if any leaders were more secure on their thrones. Virtually anyone with any power in Mexico owed his position to Díaz's largesse. Even the people who were unable to vote accepted Díaz; he was, after all, honest—something that could not be said for most of the sycophants who surrounded him. If he were not in power, far worse could be found. The rest of the world, growing rich on its Mexican investments, considered Díaz a great man. The United States alone had two billion dollars

*Francisco Madero challenged the Díaz dictatorship and called for free elections. When Madero was nominated for president in 1910, he was arrested and jailed on trumped-up charges by Díaz.*

## One Point of View

invested in Mexico. What might happen to that investment and those of other nations should one of Díaz's grasping henchmen come to power? Díaz's continued dictatorship seemed in the best interests of all—even those few who opposed him.

Then, in 1908 the president made a terrible miscalculation. In an interview that headlined the American publication *Pearson's Magazine*, Díaz told journalist James Creelman that he would not stand for reelection in 1910. After more than thirty years in power, Díaz said, he had set Mexico on the path of progress and could now retire. Furthermore, he welcomed the formation of political parties. The interview was reprinted in its entirety within a month in Mexico.

Historians have pondered Díaz's purpose in making such a statement. Was he simply posturing as a friend to democracy? Did he hope to lure opponents into the open? Hints at his possible retirement in the past had brought an outpouring of protests from all sides. This time such pleas did not appear. Two months after his announcement of imminent retirement appeared in the Mexican press, Díaz allowed his sycophants to persuade him that the future of Mexico depended on his continued presidency. He announced that he would indeed run for reelection in 1910 after all. No doubt he was not very hard to convince. But the damage had been done: His earlier announcement had brought out political opposition for the first time in his reign.

The name that was soon on everyone's lips was Francisco Indalécio Madero, a *hacendado* from the northeastern state of Coahuila. Balding, barely five feet two inches, and frail, Madero was hardly an inspiring figure physically. When making speeches, his high-pitched voice tended to rise to a falsetto. Furthermore, as the eldest son in a family that owned nearly four million acres as well as mines, factories, and other businesses, he seemed an unlikely reformer.

But Madero had been educated in

France, where he learned to appreciate democratic principles. He showed his concern by working to improve the lives of the peons on his own lands by improving living conditions and raising wages. Such actions made him unpopular with neighboring *hacendados*. He even built schools and paid the teachers out of his own pocket.

In 1908 he burst on the nation's political scene by writing a book, *The Presidential Succession of 1910*. It was anything but a call to arms. In fact, Madero specifically ruled out revolution as a method for change. He praised Díaz as a person but criticized the dictatorship. The way to Mexico's improvement, he argued, lay in free elections open to all and an end to continued reelections of the president. The book immediately became a best-seller. Madero became the spokesman for the Anti-Reelectionist Party. In April 1910 he was nominated for president.

At first Díaz and his coterie regarded Madero's challenge with amused tolerance. When the aged dictator met with Madero, he promised free and fair elections. But as Madero began to draw larger and more enthusiastic crowds, the Díaz crowd began to take him seriously. In June the candidate was jailed on trumped-up charges and kept there until the election was over. To practically no one's surprise it was announced that President Díaz had won reelection by an overwhelming majority.

Díaz's high-handed treatment of Madero brought about a turning point in Pancho Villa's life. One of Madero's strongest supporters was Abraham González in the state of Chihuahua. Convinced that Díaz could not be toppled by peaceful means, González began looking for men to lead a revolution. He arranged a meeting with Villa, where he explained to the bandit leader what Madero stood for and what he hoped to accomplish for the poor. Villa was particularly impressed to learn that Madero had gone to prison for

## Dirty, Vicious, and Lazy

*The view of the Díaz regime toward its subjects—those it supposedly worked for—was stated by Charles C. Cumberland in* Mexico: The Struggle for Modernity.

"Mexico had untold wealth, the land produced marvelously, and the great mass of the people, particularly the Indians, in their worthlessness held up progress. The mass of the population, according to most official doctrine after about 1880, could not and would not work efficiently, they were dirty and vicious and lazy, they had to be taught obedience, they would not save money because they were drunkards, and whatever wage they received was probably more than their productivity deserved."

*Uneducated and unworldly, Emiliano Zapata became one of Mexico's most famous revolutionaries. He and his army controlled the area south of Mexico City for nearly a decade.*

opposing Díaz. He was given a captain's commission and promised González he would recruit soldiers for the revolution.

Madero was now also convinced that the only way to bring political change in Mexico was through revolution. He jumped bail in the central state of San Luis Potosí in October and fled north. He set up headquarters in San Antonio, Texas, where he issued a manifesto declaring the recent election void, naming himself provisional president, and promising a free presidential election as well as a revision of the unfair laws and decrees of the Díaz regime as soon as Díaz was driven out. To avoid complications with the United States over fomenting revolution in Mexico while living in Texas, the mani-

festo was backdated to Madero's last day in Mexico and called the Plan of San Luis Potosí.

The revolution began ineptly. A couple of spontaneous uprisings cost some enthusiasts their lives. Madero had provided the spark and inspiration for the revolution, but he was no military man. In mid-November he crossed the border into Mexico, expecting to meet a small body of three hundred armed supporters and attack the border town of Piedras Negras. Only about twenty-five men arrived, and the arms and ammunition Madero had purchased never showed up at all. Discouraged, the provisional president returned to San Antonio. A week later Díaz issued a statement that although there had been "a few mutinies of small importance," they had been suppressed. "The political situation in Mexico does not present any danger."

He was wrong, of course. Madero in San Antonio could not yet see the dawn, but all over Mexico hope was rising.

## Villa Begins the Revolution

The revolution brought together all those with grievances against the Díaz regime. The stated aims of Madero's Plan of San Luis Potosí were not necessarily those of everyone who joined him. They were united only in their opposition to Díaz. At one extreme were those who wished only for a change in the personnel of government; they would be satisfied simply to replace the Porfirians with themselves. At the other end of the spectrum were those who wanted a complete change in the social structure of the country; they ex-

*Former mule driver and storekeeper Pascual Orozco was one of the most successful rebel army leaders of the revolution.*

American-born Pascual Orozco, a tall, thin mountaineer, had been a mule driver and storekeeper. Somehow this prepared him to become an effective general, who led victorious rebel armies in the most important fighting of the revolution.

Pancho Villa was the third important military leader. It was Villa who gave the revolution its first victory—and none too soon. A deeply discouraged Madero was on the verge of giving up the struggle and sailing in exile to Europe when word arrived that Villa, with a force of five hundred men he had culled from the desert had captured the small town of San Andrés near Chihuahua. Soon after came the news that Orozco had taken the larger town of Guerrero to the south. Neither town had been held—the rebels were not yet that strong—but the temporary victories proved that the Mexican army could be beaten. And that awareness brought a flood of new converts to the rebel side.

Meanwhile, the Mexican army was hardly an army. Reportedly thirty thousand strong, it could marshal only eighteen thousand men at best. Deserters, disabled, and even deceased were still carried on the roles so that dishonest officers could embezzle their pay. Of those soldiers who were actually present and in uniform, many had been conscripted against their will, and most had been brutally treated. They were not likely to fight to the last man to preserve the Díaz regime, especially since most of the officers who cheated and mistreated them owed their appointments not to any military skill, but to favoritism from the Porfirians. Mexican army soldiers captured during the revolution were usually given the chance to join the rebels. Captured officers were shot.

pected all power, wealth, and land to be redistributed. Although most of Madero's followers fell somewhere between those two poles, some joined the revolution merely for adventure or for booty.

Three important military leaders emerged for the revolutionaries. In the south Emiliano Zapata led an army made up mostly of Indian farmers. "He was a man of no learning, of no broad social contacts, a simple, vigorous human being," wrote historian Frank Tannenbaum, "who knew that his people had been robbed of their lands, and that it was his call to return these lands to them." [23] For nearly a decade Zapata and his Army of the South controlled the area south of Mexico City.

Most of the fighting came as skirmishes and hit-and-run raids. In some of the border towns Americans came out to watch the fighting across the way while refreshments were sold. Although a few onlookers were killed by stray shots from the Mexican side, the "tea battles" proved popular entertainment.

Villa became known as the most dashing of the northern generals, but his propensity for cruelty also became part of his reputation. For some reason Villa particularly hated Chinese. When he wanted to insult an American, he would call him a *chino blanco*, a "white Chinese." The city of Torreón had a large Chinese population; they had drifted south from California after the gold rush sixty years earlier. A dispute over some meals served to Villistas in a Chinese restaurant led to the slaughter of two hundred Chinese, many by torture.

Because the Chinese distrusted banks, their valuables were usually found in their homes. The Villistas looted these, realizing a profit from their racial prejudice.

In Mexico City Díaz had at first ignored and then sneered at the revolution. But even he had to finally admit that the rebels were winning. By April 1911 he went before the Mexican congress and admitted that his government was helpless to stop the rebels. Some of his advisors urged him to resign; others made their feelings known by leaving the country. Díaz was willing to concede that he favored no more reelections after he had served out this, his eighth, term.

The most important battle began on April 19 with a truce. The rebel forces assembled to the west of Ciudad Juárez, across the border from El Paso. Americans turned out for the show, but to their dis-

*Villa (center) achieved the revolution's first victory when he and his rebel force of five hundred temporarily captured the town of San Andrés.*

appointment, there was none. Villa, Orozco, and most other rebel officers favored an attack, but Madero believed he could negotiate a bloodless surrender with eighty-year-old Juan Navarro, one of the most hated of Díaz's generals. Navarro had earlier presided at a federal victory, after which not only were all rebel soldiers shot, but also all suspected sympathizers. To the exasperation of Villa and the others, Madero proclaimed a ten-day truce so that negotiations could take place. When nothing was resolved after ten days, the truce was extended five more.

On May 7 Madero announced that he intended to abandon the siege and move south. Although by now the rebels held both numerical strength and superior arms, Madero claimed to be afraid that fighting might bring casualties on the El Paso side of the border, which might lead to American intervention on behalf of the Federales, or federal troops. The next morning the El Paso *Times* was delivered to the rebel camp. It contained a quotation from Navarro's second in command, accusing the rebels of cowardice.

That was too much for Villa. Along with Orozco, he ordered some of his men to make provocative advances toward Ciudad Juárez. As he expected, they drew fire, and the battle was on. Later Villa readily admitted that he had circumvented Madero's truce. As justification, he added, "Sometimes a civilian chief is unable to see what is plain to the eyes of his military subordinate. If the success of a campaign or a revolution is at stake, the subordinate must be guided by his own judgment."[24]

Two days after it began, the battle ended with Navarro's surrendering his sword. Out of Navarro's original contingent of 500 men, 180 had been killed, and 250 wounded; rebel losses were higher yet, but they had started with six times as many troops. Five Americans were killed by stray bullets on the El Paso side of the border; Washington grumbled diplomatically but took no action, much to Madero's relief.

The execution of General Navarro seemed certain, but in an act of foolhardy gallantry, Madero borrowed a car, drove the old man to the home of the German consul, and released him. When Villa and Orozco learned of Navarro's escape, they attempted to arrest Madero at gunpoint.

Somehow Madero was able to convince them he had done the right thing. The whole incident ended with embraces all around and an emotion-choked Villa in tears.

The armies of the revolution in the north under Villa and Orozco and in the south under Zapata advanced on the capital, usually with little resistance from dispirited federal troops. At last even Díaz recognized his cause as hopeless. He was spirited out of Mexico City and on to Veracruz, where he boarded a German steamer on May 31, 1911. The onetime dictator did not, as so many other deposed autocrats have done, take with him the national treasury. Power, not wealth, had always been his goal. He lived out his remaining days in simplicity in Paris, dying of natural causes on July 2, 1915.

His departure was celebrated by most in Mexico; those who felt differently said nothing. Foreign observers had mixed reactions. Perhaps the most hostile and possibly the most accurate assessment of Díaz came from John Kenneth Turner who wrote:

> He built a machine, enriched his friends and disposed of his enemies, buying some and killing others. He flattered and gifted the foreigner, favoured the Church, kept temperance in his body, and learned a martial carriage; he set one friend against another, fostered prejudice between his people and other peoples, . . . cried in the sight of the multitude when there was no sorrow in his soul—and wrecked his country.[25]

# Chapter

# 4 Another Turn in the Wind

When Francisco Madero and Porfirio Díaz met before the 1910 election, Madero urged the aged dictator to relinquish his power voluntarily:

> "Into whose hands do you counsel me to give it?" asked Díaz.

> "Into the hands of an honest man," was the reply.

> "Senor," said Díaz, "a man must be more than honest to govern Mexico."[26]

Díaz was barely on his way into exile in Paris when Madero began proving the old man's prophecy accurate. Madero was certainly an honest man. He meant well. But he had already shown himself a weak and ineffective military leader. Now he proved to be an inept politician.

Even a master politician would have had his hands full steering through Mexico's political scene. When the common enemy had been Díaz, the various revolutionary factions had pulled together; but once Díaz was unseated, they splintered into many different groups, each with its own prescription for saving Mexico. Some looked for only modest changes; others pushed for complete land reform. Should foreign investment continue to be encouraged? Or should some Mexican industries

be nationalized? Moreover, many of the old Díaz supporters were still around, hoping to put a new Díaz on the throne. Ironically, although the Porfirians had lost

*Although honest and well intentioned, Madero's weak political skills prevented him from realizing his vision for Mexico.*

the revolution, they still controlled the army and much of the legislature. Madero tried to bring all of these opposites together into one unified government. As usual he bent over backwards to placate his enemies and only succeeded in enraging his friends. One of his first moves was to appoint Francisco de la Barra as provisional president. Described as "a marshmallow made up to look like a man," de la Barra had been a career diplomat under Díaz.[27] His appointment brought any revolutionary progress by the government to a screeching halt. Madero was Mexico's leader, but de la Barra had the power.

A constant thorn in Madero's side was Henry Lane Wilson, the American ambassador to Mexico. Wilson, a fifty-five-year-old career diplomat, had admired Díaz—particularly the way the old dictator catered to American business interests. In 1911 Wilson had advocated American intervention to help Díaz crush the revolution. Once Madero took office in September 1911, Wilson bombarded Washington with criticisms of the new president and his government's instability. With so much hostility flowing from their representative in Mexico, President William Howard Taft's administration could only look on Madero with mistrust.

Not only was Madero's government pulled in every direction by differing philosophies, there were more than enough opportunists on all sides who put personal ambition above the needs of their country. Pascual Orozco was one of the most dangerous. He had expected to be made rich and powerful by the new government. When he was appointed to the relatively minor role of military commander in the state of Chihuahua, he smoldered with resentment.

*Career diplomat Francisco de la Barra (left) was named provisional president by Madero, an act that halted revolutionary progress.*

Pancho Villa, on the other hand, was satisfied that the revolution had triumphed. His reward was simply that he had become legitimate. Once Madero was safely ensconced in Mexico City, Villa returned to Chihuahua City and entered the meat business. He married his sweetheart, Luz Corral, and appeared ready to settle down to a quiet life as a middle-class businessman. Had Madero somehow been able to make his vision of Mexico work, history might have heard no more of Pancho Villa.

In the south Emiliano Zapata waited impatiently for the promised land reform that had led him into revolution in the first place. He became concerned when the government began to demobilize the rebel army in favor of the remnants of the discredited regular army. When Zapata balked at disarming his men, Madero traveled south to Cuernavaca to convince him. Although disarmament was no doubt against his better judgment, Zapata was impressed by Madero's sincerity. When Madero offered to pay each Zapatista ten dollars to turn in his rifle, Zapata agreed.

Madero seemed to have triumphed, but the crusty de la Barra, still provisional president and in power, ruined everything. Instead of negotiating with Zapata, he announced that it was "truly disagreeable that an individual with antecedents such as his should be permitted to maintain such an independent attitude."[28] De la Barra sent a force under the command of General Victoriano Huerta, a bitter enemy of Zapata's, to disarm the Zapatistas by force if necessary. Zapata reacted as one would expect, and his men kept their rifles. Once more Madero negotiated a compromise with Zapata, only to have de la Barra short-circuit the agreement by reinforcing Huerta and ordering him to go forward with disarming the Zapatistas.

Soon fighting broke out. At last Madero succeeded in having Huerta replaced as federal commander. That quieted the fighting but gained Madero a dangerous enemy in the ousted general.

## Rebellion Returns

Madero retained the loyalty of the masses and won an overwhelming victory for the presidency in the free elections held in 1911, but he was quickly adding opponents among the powerful: the old Díaz people, the Catholic Church, big business, foreign investors, and some segments of the revolutionary group, to say nothing of such loose cannons as Huerta and Orozco. Even in winning the election, Madero made new enemies by choosing José Pino Saurez, a journalist who had played no part in the revolution, as his vice presidential running mate over the better claim of Dr. Francisco Vázquez Gómez, one of the revolution's leaders. In the south Zapata was still up in arms. Madero offered him freedom if he would surrender; Zapata countered with an extreme land reform plan: all foreign-owned lands and property to be confiscated, half the land of hacienda owners friendly to the revolution to be divided among the people, and hacienda owners opposed to the revolution to lose all.

A compromise might have been possible; both men respected each other. But then Madero made another tragic miscalculation and appointed as governor of the region a man who owned huge tracts of land and who was completely unacceptable to Zapata. The new revolution in the south continued.

Soon there was fighting in the north. Early in 1912 supporters of Dr. Gómez rebelled in Chihuahua, accusing Madero of being untrue to his own plan of San Luis Potosí. In March they were joined by Pascual Orozco, who brought six thousand troops and vast quantities of military supplies into the fray. The government, tied down by Zapata in the south and several other minor rebellions, was unable to keep Orozco from occupying nearly all of Chihuahua.

At last Orozco received some opposition, but not from the government. Pancho Villa remained loyal to Madero; at the same time, he blamed Orozco for talking him into the abortive attempt to arrest Madero because of General Navarro's escape. Villa abandoned his meat business and raised a small army of about five hundred men. He attacked the mining town of Parral in Chihuahua, announcing: "If you are loyal to the government come out and receive me, and if you are an enemy, come out and fight. I shall take the town in any case." He captured the town unopposed, fought off an attack by Orozco's troops, and when a larger Orozco army forced his withdrawal, he left the town

General Victoriano Huerta was commissioned by de la Barra to disarm the Zapatistas. He was replaced as federal commander before he could carry out the objective.

with seventy thousand dollars of the local businessmen's money.

Orozco's men, called *colorados* by the Mexicans, set new standards for cruelty in the towns they savaged. They seemed to enjoy inflicting pain and death merely for the joy of it. Even Villa, certainly no stranger to cruelty himself, found the *colorados'* treatment of the native population unforgivable. *Colorados* captured by Villa were always shot.

Villa was able to win a number of skirmishes, but he did not have the manpower to meet Orozco in a major battle. When Madero's government was finally able to send a sizable army north, it blundered into a massacre. Madero grudgingly sent General Victoriano Huerta with another army. Huerta was a drunkard who began imbibing, or drinking, from the moment he rose in the morning and continued through the day, yet somehow he was also a competent general.

Villa immediately allied his men to Huerta's army, but cooperation was doomed from the start. Villa rode into Huerta's camp dusty and dirty from his journey. He was confronted by Huerta's elaborately uniformed officers, who immediately sneered at the scruffy newcomer dressed in old clothes. They further angered Villa by denigrating, or belittling, his military ability: They called him "honorary general" as though he had no right to lead. Huerta, for his part, demanded absolute obedience; he decided the independent Villa was violent, undisciplined, and totally unreliable. Tensions mounted.

In July, when Villa refused to turn over to the army some horses captured in a raid, Huerta had him arrested in the middle of the night, tried for insubordination, and sentenced to be shot at dawn. In the morning Villa was stood against a wall opposite a firing squad. He was handing out his watch and money to the soldiers when one of Huerta's officers arrived with a temporary stay of execution he had wheedled out of the general. Shortly after that a permanent stay arrived from Madero. Under heavy guard Villa was taken to a military prison in Mexico City. He made good use of his time, enlisting a young clerk to teach him the rudiments, or basics, of reading and writing.

While Villa sat in prison, Huerta drove Orozco back with victory after victory until the rebel was forced to flee into exile in the United States. Huerta returned to Mexico City a hero, even though it soon became clear that he had embezzled seven hundred thousand dollars during his campaign. When Madero questioned him about the missing money, he blandly remarked, "I am no bookkeeper."

## The Fall of Madero

Villa remained in prison until Christmas Day, when with a little help from friends, he simply walked out, disguised in a hat and dark glasses. He made his way north, crossed the border, and settled down in El Paso. He was still loyal to Madero and sent

---

### In Spite of That. . .

*In* Memoirs of Pancho Villa, *Villa marveled at General Huerta's drinking habits.*

"If his judgment is sometimes at fault it is only because he begins to drink by seven in the morning and is hardly ever at his best. Not once in all the times I spoke to him was he altogether sober, for he drank morning, afternoon and night. His talents must have been very great."

---

*Earth soaked with Madero's blood is recovered from the site where the president was slain. The details of the February shooting of Madero and former vice president Pino Suarez remain unclear.*

word when he learned of yet another plot against the president. Madero's men thanked him and even sent him money but asked that he stay in exile so as not to compromise the president.

Madero's government was faltering badly. Even the common people who had always supported him were turning away, for he was unable to put through any of the badly needed reforms in land ownership, schooling, or wages. He still hoped for the best, but he was too weak to accomplish it. Two army generals who had led unsuccessful revolts against him would have been summarily, or immediately, shot by any other Mexican leader; Madero had them placed in prison, where they continued to foster revolt.

He was warned of an impending coup by a group of officers, including the two in prison. One of the men listed as a conspirator was General Huerta. However, there was a question mark after Huerta's name, and Madero decided this meant that the list was false. In early February 1913 fighting began in Mexico City. Soldiers loyal to Madero held off the rebels, but the general charged with protecting the government was wounded and had to be replaced. Incredibly, Madero put Huerta in charge.

Although the coup attempt seemed on the verge of defeat when Huerta took over, the fighting dragged on for ten days. A great number of civilians were killed, but Huerta made little progress against the rebels. He had no intention of doing so; he was part of the coup and was simply waiting for the right moment when the people of the capital would be so sick of fighting that they would welcome a new government. In the meantime he did what he could to set the stage. One company of soldiers known to be loyal to Madero was ordered to charge the rebels across open ground. Naturally, they were slaughtered almost to the man.

At noon on February 18 Madero was arrested by officers who had thrown in with Huerta. That afternoon, cheered by a large crowd, Huerta appeared on the balcony of the presidential palace and declared that peace had come. "Mexico has been saved," rhapsodized American ambassador Henry Lane Wilson, whose hatred for Madero bordered on pathological, or mentally diseased. The next evening Gustave Madero, the president's brother, was shot "while attempting to escape."

Three days later, while Americans celebrated Washington's birthday, Francisco Madero and his former vice president, José Pino Saurez, were gunned down. The report of their attempted escape was so clumsily handled that only the most credulous, or gullible, would put any stock in it. Supposedly, Madero and Pino Saurez were being moved to a different prison when a dozen men attempting to free them fired on the car they were riding in! Then Madero and Pino Saurez leaped from the car and ran toward the men who were shooting and were killed by those who had come to rescue them. Such a scenario, calling for the collective lunacy of Madero, Pino Saurez, and the reputed rescuers, was dismissed by nearly everyone except Henry Lane Wilson, who cabled Washington: "I am disposed to accept the government's version of the affair." However, an autopsy showed that Madero had been executed with a single bullet to the back of his head.

## The Revolution Continues

Opposition to Huerta came quickly. A senator, Dr. Belisario Dominguez, delivered a strong anti-Huerta speech to the legislature. His bullet-riddled body was found a few days later.

Emiliano Zapata, already in revolt in the south, increased his efforts. In the north the opposition was led by an unlikely revolutionary. Venustiano Carranza, the fifty-four-year-old governor of the state of Coahuila in northern Mexico, was a tall, aloof landowner who had served as a senator under Díaz before joining Madero's revolution. He affected a magnificent handlebar mustache and flowing white beard parted in the middle and wore blue-tinted spectacles to protect his weak eyes. Although he little knew or understood the ordinary people of his country, he never doubted that he was the only one who could save them.

He followed the traditional revolutionary pattern of publishing a manifesto of objections and objectives. On March 26, 1913, he revealed his Plan of Guadalupe, a document sufficiently vague to appeal to virtually anyone with a complaint against the Huerta government. Its only real specifics were its denial of Huerta's legitimacy as president and the appointment of Carranza himself as "First Chief of the Constitutionalists."

Although Carranza had his virtues, military ability was not one of them. His forces, badly led, were consistently beaten back in Coahuila by federal troops. More formidable opposition to Huerta was led in Sonora in northwestern Mexico by Alvaro Obregón, a thirty-three-year-old rancher with an organizational genius. Obregón traced his ancestry back to an Irishman named O'Brien, who had served as a bodyguard to Spanish viceroys, or governors, in Mexico a hundred years earlier. He lacked military training but surrounded himself with competent officers and listened to their opinions before acting.

In Washington Woodrow Wilson had succeeded Taft as president. He looked with horror at Madero's murder. The biased Henry Lane Wilson was removed as ambassador to Mexico and not replaced, as the American government refused to recognize Huerta as the legitimate ruler of Mexico. Instead, Woodrow Wilson tilted toward Carranza if only because of the first chief's announced intention to return his country to a constitutional government.

*In his Plan of Guadalupe, Coahuila governor Venustiano Carranza criticized the Huerta government and appointed himself "First Chief of the Constitutionalists."*

# The Centaur of the North

On March 13, on horses stolen in El Paso, Pancho Villa and eight followers splashed across the Rio Grande to join the fight against Huerta. He sent a bold message to Huerta's general in Chihuahua: "Knowing that the government you represent was preparing to extradite me I have saved them the trouble. I am now in Mexico, ready to make war upon you." The general attempted to buy him off with an offer of fifty thousand dollars and an appointment as a general in the federal army. Villa suggested what Huerta could do with the money and added, "I do not need the rank as I am already supreme commander of free men."[29]

Villa's name was magic. By summer seven hundred men had flocked to his Division of the North. Many brought with them their wives and even children, so that in transit his force looked less like an army than like wandering refugees. Nevertheless, under Villa they proved effective fighters. Some of the women fought beside their men; they were called *soladera*.

Villa supported his army by using his old standbys, rustling and extortion. Most of his troops were impoverished peons who came in from haciendas and small towns, but there was a sprinkling of educated volunteers. Also in the ranks were adventurers, soldiers-of-fortune, criminals, and some outright monsters. Rudolfo Fierro became known as the revolution's most ruthless killer. After one victory he personally executed three hundred *colorados*. Only an aching trigger finger kept the total from climbing higher.

With cutthroats like Fierro around, Villa had to be ever alert to assassination attempts. He never slept where he first announced he would; he never ate a regular meal but would move among his soldiers in seeming camaraderie, or friendliness, taking a bite here and another there. His best defense was his own reputation as a crack marksman; would-be assassins knew that if they missed with their first shot, they would not get a second.

*Merciless killer Rudolfo Fierro (third from left, standing by Villa) once single-handedly murdered three hundred of Orozco's men.*

On one occasion Villa's suspicion led to tragedy. A young lieutenant, having completed a mission, reported to Villa. Suddenly he made a quick move toward his hip pocket. Villa, suspecting a gun or knife, drew his revolver and fired, killing the young man. When they looked in his hip pocket, they found only a handkerchief. The poor fellow had only had to sneeze.

Villa was willing to accept Carranza as first chief—he would have pledged allegiance to anyone opposing Huerta—but the two were so temperamentally dissimilar that the alliance could never outlast their mutual opposition to Huerta. They were like fire and ice. Villa showed his feelings with every word or gesture; he could never understand the aloof Carranza. For his part, Carranza viewed Villa as an unreliable, emotion-ruled powder keg.

In the United States opinions of Villa varied. In some circles he was the romantic savior of his country; in others he was a murderous outlaw. The anti-Villa opinions received a boost from the circumstances surrounding the death of William S. Benton, a Scotsman who had lived in Mexico for thirty years and grown rich in the

## Temper Tantrum

*Villa's sudden explosions were well chronicled. Ronald Atkin in* Revolution! Mexico 1910–1920 *presents some examples:*

"Even Villa's own troops suffered from his erratic temper. On one occasion annoyed by the yells of a drunken soldier while he [Villa] was being interviewed by an American journalist, Villa casually pulled his pistol and killed the man from the window, without interrupting his conversation.

Villa's temper was also demonstrated violently when Patrick O'Hea went to the rebel chief with a complaint that his house, near the railway just outside of Torreon, was being shot up by trigger-happy soldiers as their trains went past. Villa refused to believe the story but was persuaded to go with O'Hea to a first floor balcony of the Hotel Francia, overlooking the railway yard, as a troop train began to move out. 'Just then some presumably drunken warrior on the train, out of habit, started shooting into the air', wrote O'Hea. 'Villa threw me aside . . . jerked a weapon from a blanching guard and emptied its chambers into the humanity atop the moving caravan. I saw at least one man fall, crumbling, from the roof-top to the ground.'"

*Villa's revolutionary victories and growing fame attracted many followers. By September 1913 his army had swelled to eight thousand.*

process. Benton went to see Villa to complain about various injuries to his property committed by the Villistas. They argued, and according to Villa, Benton attempted to pull a gun and was arrested, tried, and executed. His body was buried the next morning. When a storm of protests over Villa's treatment of a foreigner burst in the United States, Villa produced an account of Benton's trial, including numerous statements by witnesses. No trial had taken place, of course, but Villa also proposed to dig up Benton's body to show he had been lawfully executed by firing squad. It was then that Rudolfo Fierro, who had been in charge of the execution, told Villa that the Scotsman had not actually been shot but had been dispatched by a blow to the head. Villa suggested exhuming the body and shooting it, but it was pointed out that any doctor could easily tell that the bullets had been fired into a dead body. Villa stalled. Finally, word came from Carranza that any further investigation by outsiders would violate Mex-

ican sovereignty and that Villa was to make no more statements about the affair without first clearing them through him. For once Villa was happy to accept an order from the first chief.

Despite such episodes opinion of Villa in the United States became, on the whole, more positive. In the overblown style of the day, he was called the Centaur of the North. If nothing else, he was regarded as morally superior to Huerta. More to the point, he was winning the revolution.

In September he captured the town of Torreón, an important federal communications center in Durango, thereby somewhat isolating other federal outposts in the state of Chihuahua to the north. By then his army had grown from the original eight with whom he had crossed the border six months before to eight thousand. An attack on Chihuahua City failed, but Villa moved against Ciudad Juárez, Mexico's most important border town, with a brilliant stratagem, or trick.

In November he took two thousand

men north. They captured a freight train that had just left Ciudad Juárez and forced the railroad telegrapher to send a message to the city that the tracks had been torn up by revolutionaries. Back came orders for the train to return. Villa secreted his men aboard the train, which then steamed unchallenged into Ciudad Juárez in the middle of the night. Villa was able to capture the city without losing a man.

The Federales sent an army large enough to fill eleven trains to recapture Ciudad Juárez, but Villa met them south of the city. On the third day of fighting, the Villistas routed the federal army with a massed cavalry charge.

Not only had Villa's Division of the North repulsed a fully equipped federal army of equal size, but also, with possession of the border city, arms and other supplies could now be funneled to the revolution from the United States. Within two weeks the Federales abandoned the state of Chihuahua to the rebels.

# 5 The Allies Fall Out

In mid-October 1913 General Huerta held a farcical election. Only a smattering of votes was cast. The general later admitted that he had wished one of the official candidates well, "but if he had been elected president I should have had him shot."[30] Although he was not an official candidate, to no one's great surprise General Huerta won in a landslide. Then, to preserve the barest appearance of legitimacy, he had the election declared void so that government control reverted to the provisional president who was, of course, Huerta.

The sham election confirmed American president Woodrow Wilson's belief that Huerta must be toppled. The United

*General Huerta (second from right) used fraud to obtain a landslide victory in the 1913 presidential election. His openly corrupt behavior convinced the United States that he must be ousted from office.*

*American soldiers file through the streets of Veracruz. The U.S. capture of Veracruz failed to topple Huerta's government.*

States still refused to recognize his government as legitimate. Arms were being sold to Carranza through Ciudad Juárez, while at the same time they were being denied to Huerta. Then, in the Gulf Coast city of Tampico, the barest wisp of a reason for U.S. intervention presented itself.

The United States had kept a considerable portion of its navy sailing around the Gulf of Mexico for years. Officially the ships were there to protect American citizens and business interests, particularly investments in Mexican oil fields. Unofficially they were there to intimidate Mexico and the Caribbean countries. In April 1914 Tampico fell under attack by rebel forces. The U.S. Navy began removing American civilians from harm's way. When a motor launch ran low on fuel, a whaleboat under the command of an inexperienced ensign was sent to one of the piers to buy gasoline. The Mexican soldiers guarding the pier had orders to keep everyone away from the pier, and they arrested the American sailors.

The sailors were released a few hours later, along with the Mexican commander's regrets. That was not good enough for the American admiral, who was looking for provocation so that he could flex American muscle. He demanded a formal apology, the punishment of the officer responsible for the arrest, and a 21-gun salute from the Mexican army. Mexico could either grovel at the feet of the American eagle or face its talons. Huerta refused to grovel. At about the same time word reached Washington that a German freighter loaded with munitions for Huerta was bound for Veracruz.

Using the Mexican insult to the American flag—the refusal of a 21-gun salute—as a pretense, three thousand American marines and sailors landed at Veracruz and occupied the city. In the fighting nineteen Americans and many more

Mexicans, including women and children, were killed.

Wilson had badly miscalculated; he had expected the capture of Veracruz to be the straw to break Huerta's back and unseat his government. Instead, Mexico reacted with violent anti-American feeling. "Vengeance, Vengeance, Vengeance!" screamed one newspaper's headline. For a time General Huerta harbored the hope that all Mexicans, including the rebels, would unite behind him to avenge the insult. Carranza would not go that far, but he did appeal to Washington to withdraw from Veracruz immediately.

Shocked by the vehemence of the Mexican reaction, Wilson issued orders that the marines go no farther into Mexico. He also stopped shipping arms to Carranza. The 21-gun salute was never delivered, of course, and the German freighter eventually dropped off Huerta's munitions farther down the coast. The only thing the landing accomplished, aside from killing and wounding, was that a number of Americans spent a hot summer in Mexico.

## Villa Resigns

By May it had become simply a question of time for Huerta. Sooner or later Pancho Villa and the Division of the North were going to march into Mexico City. Carranza decided it should be later. He feared, with good cause, that his presidential dreams would disappear should Villa's be the first rebel army into the capital.

Villa, in Torreón, was readying his troops to strike south at the mining town of Zacatecas in central Mexico. Once that stronghold was breached, the road would be open to Mexico City. Carranza arrived and ordered him to go 180 miles east and attack the city of Saltillo, 660 miles north of Mexico City, instead. The purpose behind the order was transparent. Although Saltillo posed a threat to the rebel flank, a rebel army—the Division of the Northeast—was standing by not 50 miles away. The only reason to detour Villa for the job was to keep him away from the capital. Villa understood Carranza's purpose, of course, and argued forcefully against the order. Finally, however, in the interest of harmony, he gave in.

On May 17 Villa's troops captured the small town of Paredon on the outskirts of Saltillo in a bloody battle that saw the federal troops sustain five hundred dead and twenty-five hundred wounded or captured. Three days later Saltillo gave up without a fight.

In the meantime Carranza ordered another general, one less ambitious than Pancho Villa, to take Zacatecas. Unfortunately for Carranza's master plan, Zacatecas refused to fall. Villa was back in Torreón when he received orders from Carranza to detach five thousand of his men and send them south to reinforce the rebel army besieging Zacatecas. Not only was Villa to be left twiddling his thumbs at Torreón, but he was also being told to give up a large part of his army.

Villa attempted a side step; he would take all of the Division of the North to Zacatecas. Carranza repeated his order for five thousand only. A telegraphic conversation was set up between Villa in Torreón and Carranza, who was in Saltillo. Angry messages flew back and forth, with neither man willing to budge. At last Villa's famous temper got the better of him. He

*As the revolution wreaked havoc on Mexico, a war of a much larger magnitude had captured the attention of the rest of the world—World War I, which began with the August 1914 German invasion of Belgium.*

telegraphed: "Senor, I resign command of this Division. Tell me to whom to deliver it."

Carranza was delighted to accept the resignation. His only serious rival for the presidency once Huerta was out of the way had just, in effect, shot himself in the foot. By the next day Villa had cooled down and realized he had blundered. He telegraphed a fence-mending message to Carranza, but the first chief was not about to reconsider accepting Villa's resignation. From Saltillo he ordered Villa's officers to choose a new leader. To a man they refused. Villa remained in command of the Division of the North, but Carranza no longer commanded Villa.

Now Villa led his army to Zacatecas. His total force of twenty-three thousand outnumbered the federal garrison two to one. The fighting was bitter, but the result was never in doubt. On June 23 the city fell. Nearly twelve thousand federal troops were killed or captured. Elated by his victory, Villa telegraphed Carranza as though no split had taken place.

Carranza refused to forget or forgive. He cut off all supplies to Villa. Ironically, the victory at Zacatecas had yielded great quantities of captured cannons, machine guns, rifles, ammunition, and just about everything Villa's army needed except one—coal. And without coal to power the locomotives, Villa could not move his army farther south. The Division of the North sat bogged down at Zacatecas while, with Carranza's blessing, Alvaro Obregón and his Division of the West triumphantly entered Mexico City on August 15, 1914.

Two weeks earlier Huerta had set sail for Spain.

And on August 4 World War I had begun in Europe with Germany's invasion of Belgium.

## More of the Same

All this time Zapata had been fighting Huerta in the south, but he and Carranza were not allies, despite their common foe. Each acted independently, with no communication between them. Although Zapata admired Villa, he had a much lower opinion of the first chief. For his part, Carranza, who considered Zapata a dangerous radical, had feared that the southern leader might capture Mexico City first and rob him of his triumph. Until Obregón could control the city, Carranza negotiated to have the federal troops maintain their positions—a hostile act aimed at the Zapatistas. Zapata, who had been opposing governments in Mexico City since Díaz's tenure, simply switched his opposition to Carranza.

Meanwhile, in the north fighting broke out between Carranza and Villa supporters at the border town of Nacos. Obregón traveled to Chihuahua City, where he met with Villa; then, together they went to Nacos, where they quelled the fighting, if not the hard feelings on either side. Back in Chihuahua City Villa and Obregón held several days of friendly talks on the direction of Mexico's future. Obregón returned to Mexico City barely in time to learn that further fighting had broken out in Sonora. Once more he journeyed back to Villa on a peace mission. But this time, shortly after Obregón arrived, Villa learned that the Carrancistas at Sonora had broken a truce. He flew into a rage, decided Obregón was trying to trick him, and ordered his men to "shoot this traitor!"

Before the hasty order could be acted on, Villa calmed down. Obregón sent a telegram to Sonora ordering the Carrancista officers to abide by the terms of the truce. In further talks with Villa Obregón was able to elicit the fiery leader's agreement to send a representative to a Carranza-sponsored conference

### Reasons

*Ronald Atkin talks about the Zapatistas in* Revolution! Mexico 1910–1920:

"The Zapatistas hung three bodies outside a police station, with notices above them giving the reason for their execution. One sign read 'This man was killed for being a thief', and another said, 'This man was killed for printing counterfeit money'. The third said simply 'This man was killed by mistake'."

*U.S. Marines in Veracruz. President Woodrow Wilson agreed to withdraw forces and turn the city over to Carranza when he finally promised not to harm Mexican civilians.*

in October to discuss the future of the revolution. Villa insisted, however, that Zapata be invited.

After three days Obregón departed for Mexico City. His train was barely out of Chihuahua City when word of another Carranza action sent Villa into another rage. By this time his hate for the first chief had reached such a state that virtually anything Carranza did could set Villa off. A telegram was sent ahead, and Obregón was taken off the train and brought back to face more of Villa's bluster and threats. Obregón left a second time for the capital that night, but before he finally got back to Mexico City, he had to evade an assassination attempt on the train.

Carranza's planned October conference was a bust.

By the time it was held, it had become no more than a footnote to a larger convention scheduled for a week later at the spa city of Aguascalientes, whose name means "hot waters," 364 miles north of Mexico City. The site was aptly chosen—it was on the border between the areas controlled by Carranza and Villa. Zapata sent representatives, and Villa, making a determined effort to achieve peace, made an impassioned—though some said incoherent—speech. He and Obregón embraced in a symbolic bear hug. However, Carranza refused to attend or to send a representative.

The convention was split between the Carrancistas and the Villistas, who were supported by the Zapatistas. At one point Villa proposed that he and Carranza not only withdraw from politics, but that they both commit suicide. His idea was not taken seriously, certainly not by Carranza. On November 2, after weeks of fiery speeches, the convention chose Eulalio Gutiérrez to supersede, or replace, Carranza as provisional president. Gutiérrez was an acceptable compromise candidate to the Carrancistas and the Villistas but had no political background.

The new provisional president was not acceptable to Carranza himself. He refused to step down, ignored an ultimatum from the convention, and was declared by Gutiérrez to be in rebellion. Villa was put in charge of the Army of the Convention and ordered to capture Mexico City. In the meantime Obregón, who had worked very hard to bring peace, reluctantly joined the Carrancistas. The civil war was on again.

## The United States, Villa, and Zapata

Meanwhile, seven thousand U.S. sailors and marines sat at Veracruz accomplishing nothing. Woodrow Wilson was anxious to

get them out and at the same time save as much face as possible. Carranza also wanted the Americans out. If Mexico City was to be lost to him, he needed a base for operations. And as Mexico's chief port, Veracruz's revenue in duty fees would come in handy in the newest installment of the civil war. But the fact that both sides wanted the same end did not keep the prickly Carranza from creating a roadblock.

When the Americans landed, he declared that any Mexican who cooperated with them would be shot. But of course a certain amount of cooperation was necessary if the city was to be run at all. And as months went by and relations within Veracruz were normalized, the amount of cooperation between Americans and Mexicans increased. In September Wilson agreed to withdraw his troops if Carranza gave assurances that Mexican civilians in

### Cruelty

*The degree of cruelty during the revolution was horrifying. All sides were guilty. William Weber Johnson gives a description of some of the excesses in Mexico.*

"The fighting had also a nightmare quality. Captives had the soles of their feet sliced off and were forced to run across open country until they were mercifully shot down. Some prisoners were made to attempt escape so that a revolutionary chieftain could practice his marksmanship, as cooly as a man would shoot clay pigeons. Ears were lopped off and the victims made to [dance a] jig until their hearts pumped the blood from their bodies. . . . [Men] were tied to horses' tails and dragged through cobbled streets. Men known to be innocent were hanged in order to demonstrate the seriousness of demands for money. Plantation foremen were nailed to hacienda doors and left to die."

*Villa (third from right) inspects his arsenal of rifles. Villa obtained his arms from the United States and thus was eager to maintain good relations with the country.*

Veracruz would not be harmed. Carranza refused. The impasse lingered through October. Finally in November, with the possibility looming that the United States could turn the city over to the anti-Carranza side, the stubborn first chief backed down. In late November all American forces were withdrawn. The city was handed over to the Carrancistas.

As December opened Zapata was south of Mexico City and Villa was to its north. Villa was not about to repeat Carranza's mistake of entering the capital before Zapata. On December 4 at Tacuba, just outside the city, the two great leaders met face-to-face for the first time. Villa, the larger of the two, wore a pith helmet and his usual catch-as-catch-can assortment of old clothes. Zapata, somewhat of a dandy, was smartly dressed in blue, lavender, and black clothing with silver buttons. Their conversation began tentatively until they reached the subject of Carranza. Then their mutual hatred of the first chief poured forth in animated decla-

rations. Villa, who did not drink, even agreed to seal their friendship with a glass of brandy. Afterward, as he called for a glass of water, tears rolled down his cheeks, but whether from the liquor or the emotion of the moment could not be known.

On December 6 Villa and Zapata, riding side by side, paraded with their armies into a cheering Mexico City. The next day they informed provisional president Gutiérrez of their plan to beat Carranza. Then they went their separate ways and never met again. According to their plan, Zapata was to drive straight for Veracruz; Villa was to swing north, then wheel toward Veracruz, joining Zapata on the way. It was a good plan and might have brought success had the two leaders stuck to it.

Zapata and his men had secured their home state of Morelos, but that was all they were really interested in. The prospect of conquering new and strange lands on the way north to Veracruz held

*Villa and U.S. Army chief of staff General Hugh Scott emerge from a conference. Villa so impressed Scott during their meeting that the general returned to Washington with a recommendation that the United States support the revolutionary.*

no appeal for the Zapatistas. Instead, they hunkered down in Morelos and ceased making war.

Meanwhile, Villa worried about his supply lines through Chihuahua City and Torreón. He hesitated, then decided to spend December in Mexico City. Although they had been cheered on entry, some of the Villistas and Zapatistas soon turned Mexico City into chaos. Debauchery, looting, and murder were the order of the day. Men were shot for criticizing Villa, for denouncing Zapata, for praising Carranza, for minor crimes, or for no reason at all. Reportedly, 150 men were executed in the first week after Villa and Zapata entered the city, and this rate continued through Christmas.

Gutiérrez, in a bold move, attempted to institute a government that would by-pass Carranza, Zapata, and Villa. For his trouble, he was forced to flee. The convention met again at Aguascalientes in January 1915 and—with only Villa supporters present—chose a Villista, Roque González Garza, as a new provisional president.

## Villa Charms the United States

Fighting flared again in the border town of Nacos. Several Americans north of the border were killed by stray shots fired from the Mexican side. Woodrow Wilson sent his army chief of staff, General Hugh Scott, to look over the situation. On January 7 Scott and Villa met on the international bridge between Ciudad Juárez and El Paso.

Villa was eager to preserve good relations with the United States, where he purchased his arms. Furthermore, according to Enrique Alferez, a Villista:

> He liked Americans. He had a friend who was an official for the American Smelting Company. The American Smelting Company had been friendly to Villa during the revolution. And Villa prohibited the men under his command to do any harm to any properties of the American Smelting Company.[31]

Although Villa and Scott met halfway across the bridge, Villa went more than halfway to placate the American general, agreeing to withdraw his men to the south so that Americans across the border would not be endangered. Scott told Villa that in the United States Villa was viewed as a "tiger or a wolf." Particularly horrifying to Americans, Scott said, was the practice of routinely killing prisoners. He gave Villa a U.S. Army pamphlet on the treatment of captured enemy soldiers. Villa had it translated into Spanish and distributed to his officers. Reportedly, he spared the next four thousand prisoners.

Scott was impressed. Upon his return to Washington he told Wilson that the United States should support Pancho Villa. "Villa is the real force of his country," Scott wrote. "If he continues on his

*General John Pershing (right) also gave his stamp of approval to Villa (center). Pershing described Villa as a little rough, but remained convinced that he could help Mexico.*

course, he will be considered the George Washington of Mexico."[32]

Villa received good marks from another American military man in August when he met John Pershing, the commanding general at El Paso. Historian Louis R. Saddler summed up the general's reaction to Villa: "Pershing took his lead from Scott—'Villa may be a little rough but he's being very cooperative with us and there weren't any problems.'"[33]

In view of later events there is a definite irony to Pershing's report: "You will ask me whether Villa is not as bad as the others? Perhaps he is, but he represents a better cause. And it may require for some time just such a man as Villa."[34]

With the approval of such men as Scott and Pershing, Villa became convinced that the United States would come to recognize him as the legitimate leader of Mexico.

## Celaya and León

On the battlefields 1915 began well for Villa. Several small battles were lost by his underlings, but in each case Villa himself was able to ride to the rescue to turn the results around. But in April he came up against Celaya.

At Celaya, a small town 150 miles northwest of Mexico City, Obregón had dug in and prepared to fight the first modern battle on Mexican soil. The approaches to the town were crisscrossed with irrigation ditches. To add to these impediments, or obstructions, a German officer on Obregón's staff strung miles of barbed wire and placed machine guns. These were the tactics that had already turned the war in Europe into an unprecedented bloodbath. The old method of successful warfare was for the infantry to charge against fortified positions and, when the issue hung in the balance, follow up with an all-consuming cavalry charge on horseback. Using rifles, an entrenched enemy could seldom lay down enough fire to stop a determined charge of sufficient numbers. That changed with the use of charge-slowing trenches and barbed wire and the massive wall of bullets mustered by machine guns. The advantage shifted from the attackers to the defenders.

Villa was a master of the old school. His greatest successes had been achieved with massive cavalry charges. At Celaya he began with numerical superiority—twenty-five thousand men to fifteen thousand for Obregón. He sent wave after wave of attackers against the machine guns. They were relentlessly mowed down. Estimates of Villa's losses varied. He admitted to losing thirty-five hundred, but some estimates ran as high as ten thousand.

Whatever the actual number of losses, the Division of the North never fully recovered from the slaughter at Celaya. The losses in men and equipment were staggering. Nearly as harmful was the loss to Villa's reputation of invincibility. Never before had he lost a battle to an opponent of equal size.

In June Villa again sent his men against an entrenched Obregón, this time at León. Some of his officers suggested they sit back and let Obregón do the attacking, but Villa refused, knowing that Obregón would simply wait behind his entrenchments. He said, "I am a man who came into the world to attack, and if I am defeated by attacking today, I will win by attacking tomorrow."[35] Brave words, but bravado was no match for machine guns. The Villistas were once more crushed.

Although his insistence on attacking entrenched positions head-on might seem sheer stubbornness, the truth was that Villa, like the military leaders in Europe, knew no other way to succeed. In Europe this approach led to stalemate, with long miles of trenches facing each other across no-man's-land and no change for months or even years. Such a method of fighting was unavailable to Villa because reinforcements could eventually be drawn from another part of Mexico to attack him from the rear. He was forced to try for quick success with gallant charges or retreat altogether. He tried—and lost.

Obregón also suffered a loss, his right arm, when a stray shell burst near him. In great pain and thinking he was about to die anyway, Obregón pulled his revolver, placed it against his temple, and pulled the trigger. It clicked on an empty chamber; the orderly assigned to clean his pistol had forgotten to reload it. Obregón was rushed to the hospital, and his life was saved.

# 6 Betrayed

When Woodrow Wilson ran successfully for reelection in 1916, the slogan that won the hearts of American voters was "He kept us out of war." As reports of the unprecedented slaughter taking place on the battlefields of Europe reached American

*President Woodrow Wilson's success at keeping the United States out of World War I largely contributed to his reelection in 1916.*

shores, the nation recoiled in horror. Anyone who could keep American soldiers out of the carnage was the man of the moment. Wilson, who had successfully negotiated the first two years of World War I without allowing America to be drawn into the fighting, was swept back into office.

Despite its popularity the slogan contained more than a little cynicism. While Wilson struggled to maintain neutrality, knowledgeable Americans believed that eventually he would be forced to take sides in the European dispute. Then it would be only a short step to taking up arms. Sooner or later Americans would fight across the Atlantic.

If—or more likely, when—the United States entered the European war, it was crucial that it not be hobbled with an unstable situation on its southern border. The Wilson administration wrestled with the idea of settling Mexico's civil war throughout 1915—not for any great humanitarian reason, but so it could focus its full attention on Europe. It was the devout wish of Woodrow Wilson to find a Mexican leader who could unite the country and end the fighting. Although Venustiano Carranza had a legitimate claim to leadership in Mexico, he was not Wilson's ideal choice. The haughty and intractable, or obstinate, first chief had not been reli-

*Hoping to regain the Mexican presidency, exiled General Huerta (in white) gathered support for a military coup. When Huerta moved to invade Mexico from El Paso, Texas, the United States intervened and arrested the general.*

able in protecting American lives or property and had failed to institute any of the long-promised land reforms in the areas he controlled. Wilson did not trust Carranza and continued to withhold U.S. recognition of his government. On the other hand, Pancho Villa, emotional and unpredictable, was not quite Wilson's cup of tea either. Certainly, at first glance it would have been difficult to find two more different personalities than the scholarly, reserved, former Princeton University president and the illiterate, explosive, former bandit. Yet, in one way they were remarkably similar: both were idealists willing to sacrifice themselves for the good of their people. And because his cause was perceived as superior to Carranza's, Villa was nearer to receiving the

blessings of the United States as the revolution entered 1915.

In Spain the exiled General Victoriano Huerta decided he was the man to unite Mexico. Helping to convince him was a German naval officer who visited Huerta in January 1915. Captain Franz von Rintelen offered Huerta German support in a proposed military coup to return him to the Mexican presidency. German leaders knew that supposedly neutral America was selling arms and other supplies to the British and French; soon America might ally with them against Germany. But the Germans thought that if the United States was threatened by a hostile Mexico, it would be unlikely to involve itself in Europe's war. For his part Huerta promised that once he regained power, he would declare war on the United States. That the wily dictator would have actually honored such a foolhardy promise is entirely unlikely, but for the time being it put the money to buy munitions for a coup in his hands. In April he arrived in New York and immediately began contacting former allies. One who agreed to join him was Pascual Orozco, himself in exile in El Paso. Captain von Rintelen had preceded Huerta to the United States and had already purchased eight million rounds of ammunition.

As soon as he learned that Huerta had landed in the United States, Carranza began insisting that the old dictator be extradited to Mexico. The United States was not prepared to go that far as yet, since extraditing Huerta amounted to issuing a death sentence, and up to this point Huerta had not broken any American laws. Only when he made a move toward invading Mexico, and the United States knew that was his intention, would the old general become an outlaw. The U.S. Secret Service did not know about Germany's involvement, but it was not prepared to let Huerta make the chaotic Mexican situation worse by launching an invasion from the United States. From the day his ship docked in New York, he was watched by a small army of agents.

In June Huerta left New York, telling reporters he was headed for San Francisco to see the exposition being held there. But at Kansas City he switched trains, turning south toward El Paso. His plan was to meet Orozco at Newman, Texas, a small station twenty miles before El Paso. When Huerta stepped off the train, both he and Orozco were arrested.

They were taken to El Paso, where they were released on bail but kept under strict surveillance while the U.S. government decided what to do with them. When they were faced with rearrest in July, Orozco and five companions stole some horses and fled east. Ironically, they were mistaken for bandits making an across-border raid. A posse tracked them down and all six were killed in the resulting gunfight. Only later was Orozco's body identified. Huerta submitted tamely to arrest but almost immediately became seriously ill. On January 14, 1916, he died. He was buried in El Paso next to Orozco.

## The United States Tips the Scales

In Wilson's search for a horse other than Carranza to back for the Mexican presidency, Huerta had never been a consideration. The early favorite in Washington was Pancho Villa. General Hugh Scott favored him. Wilson's first secretary of state, William Jennings Bryan, had argued for Villa, apparently because Villa, like Bryan, was a teetotaler. Bryan's successor, Robert Lansing, also pushed for Villa on the firmer ground that he was the only possible candidate except for Carranza. Wilson, however, hesitated to endorse such an

*Secretary of State Robert Lansing urged Wilson to endorse Villa's bid for the Mexican presidency, but the president refused.*

unpredictable personality as Villa. Then Villa suffered his crushing defeats at Celaya and León. The view from the United States was that he was finished.

That left Carranza. At a U.S.-sponsored conference on the Mexican problem that opened in Washington in August 1916, representatives from Argentina, Brazil, Chile, Bolivia, Uruguay, and Guatemala accepted Lansing's proposal that the secondary Mexican chiefs be called on to choose a government that would exclude both Carranza and Villa. Nothing came of it. Nor could Carranza be lured into promising religious freedom, land reform, amnesty for political opponents, protection of foreigners, or recognition of their property claims as a price for American recognition of his government. By then the first chief was back in control in Mexico City, and his army was winning over Villa in the north. He was not of a mood to promise anything.

In truth, he did not have to.

On October 19 the United States extended recognition to the Carranza government as the legitimate government of Mexico. Other countries around the world quickly followed suit. With the war in Europe looming larger in U.S. affairs, Woodrow Wilson had apparently decided to close the book on Mexico.

Wilson's recognition of the Carrancistas was not universally hailed in the United States. General Hugh Scott complained that the move "had the effect of solidifying the power of the man who had rewarded us with kicks on every occasion and of making an outlaw of the man who had helped us." Several newspapers editorialized in sympathy with Villa.

Villa was not finished. He had faded into the Sierra Madre, but he still com-

## Villa's First Meeting with Carranza

*Leon Wolfe, in his* American Heritage *article "Black Jack's Mexican Goose Chase," quotes Villa's reaction to the first chief:*

"I embraced him energetically, but with the first few words we spoke my blood turned to ice. I saw that I could not open my heart to him. . . . He never looked me in the eye and during our entire conversation emphasized our differences in origin . . . lectured me on things like decrees and laws which I could not understand. . . . There was nothing in common between the man and me."

manded a sizable force of sixty-five hundred men. When he learned the United States had embraced Carranza, he felt betrayed. "I am not responsible for what happens next," he warned. "Americans know that I have always made a special effort to guarantee their safety in my country. Now, only history can decide who is responsible."[36]

He was, however, desperately short on ammunition and guns. In addition to recognizing Carranza as Mexico's legitimate leader, the United States also placed an embargo on military supplies to any Mexican faction, or group, other than Carranza. Now Villa could no longer legally buy guns and ammunition in American border towns.

"The price then skyrockets," historian Louis R. Saddler explained. "He doesn't have any money. He is out of anything he can barter—cattle, ore, cotton. Now everything he has to do in the United States is illegal. And that automatically doubles the price again. So he is doubly frustrated."[37]

Badly in need of supplies, from armaments to food, Villa planned to capture the Mexican border town of Agua Prieta, where he expected to find a small Carranza garrison. In addition to the supplies to be "liberated" there, Agua Prieta, just across the border from Douglas, Arizona, could serve as an entry point where he could deal with U.S. traders for illegal arms and supplies.

The route through the mountains was hard. Streams were swollen by autumn rains. Men and pack animals drowned. Food ran short, and some of the pack animals had to be slaughtered. Mud and rock slides took a toll. Nevertheless, as October ended, Villa arrived at Agua Prieta with a force sufficient to defeat the garrison he expected to find there. But the United States had once again intervened. Incredibly, President Wilson had allowed Carranza to transport five thousand troops by train across U.S. soil to reinforce Agua Prieta. Villa's tired and hungry men faced a far stronger enemy than they had anticipated.

They also faced a shrewd commander, who had learned the lessons of Celaya and León. Deep ditches and electrified barbed wire surrounded the town. Machine guns covered every approach. The little town had become an impregnable fortress.

On November 1 Villa opened his attack on Agua Prieta with a bombardment from his two cannons. He was careful to set up one to the east of the town and one to the west, rather than risk firing from the south and having a shell overshoot into Douglas. Despite all that had happened, he still wanted to avoid any injury to the United States. After shelling the town, he sent his men forward in a full cavalry charge, the same strategy that had proved disastrous at Celaya. Once more men and horses became embroiled in the ditches and barbed wire, and the merciless machine guns slaughtered them. If Villa had not learned how to attack a modern entrenched position, he was not alone. The famous generals of Europe were equally at a loss, though that did not keep them from sending wave after wave of attackers to almost certain death. It was not until the development of the tank that European military leaders found a way to successfully attack prepared positions.

That night Villa learned another lesson in modern warfare. He attempted to attack under cover of darkness, only to have the battlefield suddenly illuminated by giant search lights. Once more the Villistas were decimated. Ironically, the power to run the lights came from across the border in the United States.

Badly beaten as much by U.S. intervention as by Carranza's army, Villa retreated to Nacos to the west with three thousand survivors. Many of his men were badly wounded. An American copper company sent two doctors to help. Unfor-

*Mexican women and children fleeing Agua Prieta find refuge across the border in Douglas, Arizona. Carranza's army, strengthened by assistance from the United States, defeated the Villistas at Agua Prieta.*

*After six years of fighting, Mexican revolutionaries had taken many lives and ravaged the country.*

tunately, it was then that Villa learned that Agua Prieta had been reinforced only by the cooperation of the United States. He exploded. He accused the doctors of being spies and threatened to have them shot. They were imprisoned, and for several mornings they were hauled out for execution, only to have Villa change his mind and return them to their cells. Eventually, the copper company paid twenty-five thousand dollars in "taxes," and the doctors were released. However, they still had to cross miles of open desert, and one of them later died of exposure.

The heavy losses and multiple defeats reduced Villa's army to a few hundred by the end of 1915. His closest friend and able lieutenant, Rudolfo Fierro, died in a drowning accident. Many of the Villistas simply drifted off to return to the hacien-

das. In effect, he was back where he had started a half dozen years before—a bandit chief hiding out with his small band of followers in the mountains.

## Public Enemy

After nearly six years of war, Mexico was in a disastrous state. Roads and bridges were in disrepair. Mines and haciendas lay in ruins. People starved, while crops lay untended in the fields. Epidemics broke out. No precise estimate of the toll in human life was possible, but certainly for every death brought by a bullet many more died from natural causes such as disease or starvation.

Carranza, hoping to get his country's economy underway again, declared Villa finished and invited those foreign companies that had left Mexico during the revolution to return. The U.S. state department urged Americans to delay reentering Mexico until the situation clarified. Few paid heed to the warning.

In January 1916, eighteen American mining engineers for the Cusi Mining Company, along with their Mexican assistants, left El Paso by train with the intention of reopening a mine at Cusihuiriachic in the state of Chihuahua. They reached Chihuahua City without incident and changed trains to complete their journey. They never reached the mine.

A few hours out of Chihuahua City, the train was stopped by seventy Villistas under the command of Colonel Pablo López. They swarmed aboard the train, brandishing their Mauser rifles, and began taking money, watches, blankets, and even lunches. López announced to the

Mexicans, who were gathered in one car: "If you want to see some fun, watch us kill these gringos [foreigners]!"

Several of the American miners were shot where they sat in their railroad car. A few ran for their lives but were picked off almost as target practice as they dodged through the brush. The remaining Americans were herded outside onto the tracks and shot down. Their bodies were stripped of clothing and shoes. Seventeen of the eighteen Americans died. The only one to escape, Thomas Holmes, was one of those who had made a dash for safety. When bullets whistled by, he fell into a bush and pretended to be dead until the Villistas rode off.

Villa insisted that he should not be blamed. Although he had instructed López to stop the train, he said, the officer had far exceeded his orders. He promised that those responsible would be brought to justice. Indeed, within a few days two of Villa's officers were executed, and one of their bodies was exhibited in Ciudad Juárez. Whether either was actually involved in the train massacre is doubtful.

Carranza also expressed outrage and promised retribution. A few days later he claimed that eleven Villistas who had taken part in the massacre had been captured and executed.

On the American side of the border, there was no question that Villa was responsible. If he had not actually ordered the killings, which seemed likely, he was still in command of the perpetrators and, therefore, to blame. They hardly would have undertaken the massacre unless they believed Villa would approve. When the bodies of the murdered miners arrived in El Paso, an angry mob actually started for the border, vowing to invade Mexico and capture Villa. They were turned back at gunpoint by cooler heads. All along the border meetings, protests, and petitions called for the U.S. to send an army after the Mexican bandit. The rest of the country decried the incident but, not feeling directly threatened, generally opposed armed intervention.

"In times past," the San Francisco *Star* cautioned, "the Chinese have been robbed, assaulted and even ruthlessly murdered here in California by Americans, but there was never a demand by the Chinese that their government should invade this country."[38]

American writer George Marvin pointed out that quite a few Mexicans—he

*Now Public Enemy Number One in the United States, Villa was blamed for every act against Americans in Mexico, including the massacre of eighteen American miners.*

## Villa

*Leon Wolfe, writing in* American Heritage, *described Villa.*

"He walked in a slouch. On horseback he was grace personified. He spoke little. Usually he was expressionless, except for an occasional grin which became a sinister trademark in U.S. cartoons. He loved dancing: at one wedding he danced for thirty-six hours. 'He is the most natural human being I ever saw, natural in the sense of being nearest to a wild animal,' wrote an observer; another said that 'he was as unmoral as a wolf.' A journalist described his eyes as 'never still and full of energy and brutality . . . intelligent as hell and as merciless.' This was Francisco 'Pancho' Villa—social revolutionary, rapist, commander of cavalry, megalomaniac—the unbalanced and almost brilliant idol of northern Mexico."

set the figure at four hundred—had been killed by American lawmen along the border during the past four years without a single American being arrested. "You feel almost as though there were an open game season on Mexicans along the border," he said.[39] But few Americans were stirred by hearing of Mexican deaths.

Pancho Villa quickly became Public Enemy Number One north of the border. Every act against Americans in Mexico, be it murder, beating, robbery, rustling, or simple name-calling, was laid at Villa's door, ignoring the fact that there were many angry and armed Mexicans who had their own reasons for disliking gringos.

Through late January and into February rumors swirled about Villa's activities. He had been killed. He had been captured. He had been wounded. He had married again. He had escaped to the Pacific coast. He was readying an attack on Mexico City. He was on his way to Washington to deny personally any part in the attack on the miners.

On the night of March 9 any questions of Villa's whereabouts evaporated with his raid on Columbus, New Mexico.

# 7 General Pershing Invades

Even today, so many years after the event, historians differ over Pancho Villa's motive for attacking Columbus, New Mexico. The simplest answer, of course, was that he sought revenge from what he perceived as the United States' betrayal in supporting the Carranza government. Yet, it is hard to believe that Villa, still reeling from the defeat at Agua Prieta, would deliberately expose himself to retribution from the powerful United States simply out of pique, or resentment. Some argue that he was so in need of arms, horses, and money that he was willing to risk American rage in exchange for the loot he could obtain at Columbus. The Villistas took some cash and a large number of rifles in the raid, but most of the arms were discarded in the retreat. Some historians believe that Villa's aim in the attack was precisely to draw America into invading Mexico. They suggest that he hoped such an invasion would unite Mexicans behind his cause, expose the weakness of the Carranza government, and ultimately topple it. Such a course seems unusually devious for Villa, but if bringing the American army into Mexico was any part of Villa's thinking, he certainly succeeded.

U.S. newspapers called for armed retribution. Some editors, such as William Randolph Hearst, advocated conquest:

"California and Texas were part of Mexico once. . . . What has been done in California and Texas can be done ALL THE WAY DOWN TO THE SOUTHERN BASE OF THE PANAMA CANAL AND BEYOND."[40]

A New Mexico newspaper wrote: "Mexico is a white man's land and made to be occupied by an industrious, virtuous

*Captioned "Clean-up week," this 1916 cartoon reflects America's anger at Villa and the Mexican revolutionists.*

## A Natural Leader

*In* Blood on the Border, *Clarence C. Clendenen describes Pershing:*

"Pershing was a natural leader, who wore his authority without ostentation. He was affable [friendly] in manner and had a happy faculty of putting subordinates at ease, but he was merciless with the inefficient or anybody who did not render a satisfactory performance of duty. He demanded and received unwavering loyalty from his subordinates and exact compliance with his orders. From the very start of the Punitive Expedition the impact of his personality and authority was felt in every unit—even in those that were located far from his headquarters and his personal observation. It is hardly accidental that the expedition of 1916 is usually referred to as 'Pershing's Punitive Expedition.'"

and warlike race. If an inferior and unworthy race now possesses the land, they are but tenants."[41]

Joseph Pulitzer's New York *World* was less aggressive and less racist but declared, "Nothing less than Villa's life can atone for the outrage."[42]

To handle the anticipated flood of volunteers, army recruiting stations were hurriedly set up in the United States. Banners flew above them: "Help catch Villa." Surprisingly, most young Americans felt it would be more fun to read about someone else catching Villa. Instead of an expected deluge of 20,000 volunteers, 1,269 trickled in. Congress quickly passed a bill authorizing President Wilson to expand the regular army to maximum war strength, even though the administration was adamant that its plans did not include an act of war.

That was true. The United States intended to launch a "punitive expedition" into Mexico rather than an invasion. The difference, according to historian Leon Wolfe: "A punitive expedition is not technically an act of war, provided that the acting Power is strong and civilized, while the chastized nation is backward and weak."[43] Because Mexico was not a world-class power, Villa's raid on Columbus could not ever be considered a punitive expedition; meanwhile, the strong, civilized and oh-so-powerful United States was not acting as an aggressor—and any Mexican who said differently was liable to get hurt. This was all very clear to Americans; somehow Mexicans did not quite follow the logic.

Within a week of the raid on Columbus, the United States had assembled a large invading army on the border under the command of General John J. "Black Jack" Pershing.

*An experienced and skilled officer, General Pershing was chosen to lead the punitive expedition in 1916.*

## Soldier on Horseback

John Joseph Pershing was one of the greatest soldiers ever produced in the United States. His finest accomplishment came during World War I, when he led the American Expeditionary Force to Europe and to victory. After the war he was raised to the highest rank ever given an American army officer: General of the Armies of the United States.

At the time of the punitive expedition into Mexico, Pershing was still outranked by several U.S. officers, including Major General Frederick Funston, the southwestern commander. However, army chief of staff Hugh Scott recommended Pershing

to lead the expedition. It was not the first time Black Jack had been leapfrogged in rank. Funston apparently took Pershing's assignment in good grace, merely observing to reporters, "John's up against a lot." That would prove to be a classic understatement.

Born in 1840 near Laclede, Missouri, Pershing was graduated from West Point, the U.S. Military Academy, in 1886. Commissioned into the cavalry, he took part in the fighting against the Apaches and Sioux in the Southwest and while serving as a military instructor at the University of Nebraska, earned a law degree. When the Spanish-American War began in 1898, he was teaching tactics back at West Point. He distinguished himself during that war while fighting in Cuba, where his commanding officer called him "the coolest man under fire I ever saw." After the war he was sent to the Philippines, where he helped quell a revolt among the Moro people. His nickname, Black Jack, stemmed from his once having commanded a company of African-American soldiers.

Discouraged by the slow pace of promotion—he was still a lieutenant at age forty—he considered resigning from the army. However, his work in the Philippines came to the attention of President Theodore Roosevelt, and as a result he was promoted to captain and assigned as military attaché to Japan. With the outbreak of the Russo-Japanese War in 1904, he was able to study modern warfare tactics first hand. In 1906 Roosevelt promoted him all the way from captain to brigadier general, passing him over 862 senior officers.

"Pershing was not charming," one historian wrote,

nor was it his job to be charming. He was severe but fair, tall, slender, gray-haired, immaculately tailored, well-modulated in speech. He lived by a code of ethics so honorable as to be almost incomprehensible to lesser men. It is hard to imagine two humans more different than this one and Villa.[44]

For both men 1915 had been a bad year. Villa had suffered his crushing defeats at Celaya, León, and Agua Prieta. Pershing's losses were more personal: in August he received a telegram informing him that his wife and three of his children had perished in a fire that swept their home in San Francisco.

In 1916 Pershing was arguably America's most experienced officer and also its best educated in modern warfare. For the Mexican expedition he was given America's first semimodern army. The punitive expedition numbered sixty-six hundred. It included all the traditional trappings of nineteenth-century warfare—horses, mules, hard-riding riflemen, sabers, and horse-drawn cannon. But it also included the latest in battle machines and ordnance, such as three-ton trucks, tanklike armored cars, field telephone units, and eight Curtis airplanes known as Jennies.

The punitive expedition of 1916 was a demarcation for the U.S. Army between the old-fashioned horse cavalry and modern mechanized forces. Ironically, Villa's horse cavalry was better prepared for the kind of warfare that would take place.

In assembling Pershing's force within a week of Villa's Columbus raid, the army moved with unusual speed. For example,

*Members of Pershing's cavalry in Mexico ready themselves for action. Pershing's expeditionary force was supplied with the most modern warfare equipment available.*

fifty-four trucks for carrying supplies were purchased and delivered at a cost of half a million dollars. In many cases civilian drivers had to be hired until army personnel, more familiar with operating mules, could be taught to drive.

On March 15, only six days after Villa's raid, Pershing's force moved into Mexico in two columns. Pershing himself led the smaller but faster column, which departed about fifty miles to the west of Columbus. A two-thousand-strong force of cavalry and cannon, the western column hoped to catch Villa in a pincerlike movement with the larger eastern column, which included all of Pershing's supply trucks.

Pershing's written orders were to capture Villa, but it was generally believed that his unwritten instructions were to bring the Mexican bandit back dead.

## Yankee, Go Home

From the start Pershing labored under a major disadvantage. Much to the surprise of the Wilson administration in Washington, the Carranza government in Mexico City objected strenuously to having an American army ride at will all over Mexico. Earlier, Wilson had not expected Mexican objections when Americans landed at Veracruz. The American president had the unusual ability to believe in the moral correctness of his own decisions so strongly that he lost the ability to understand the view of anyone who disagreed. Early in Pershing's campaign a Carrancista officer threatened to confront the Pershing expedition with arms. Although the officer was persuaded from such a foolhardy stand, Carranza continued to

*Pershing and his aide, Lieutenant Collins, at American headquarters in Mexico. Carranza's government strongly objected to the Americans' presence in Mexico.*

complain bitterly to Washington about the invasion and to block Pershing whenever possible. He decreed that the Americans were not allowed to use any Mexican rails for troop or supply movement, forcing Pershing to rely on his unreliable trucks and Mexican roads that were sometimes no more than ruts.

Villa himself held two cards. First, the invasion was being conducted in his own backyard. Perhaps no man on earth knew the rocks and gullies of northern Mexico better than did Pancho Villa. Pershing was not simply trying to find a needle in a haystack; he was seeking a needle that

*Pershing's expedition was equipped with eight Curtis Jennies—the latest in battle machine technology. Used primarily for delivering messages back and forth, all eight were grounded because of mechanical failure.*

could move at will through the haystack. Had Pershing chosen to use his eight Jennies exclusively for scouting, he might have improved his odds of finding the needle, but they were mostly kept busy delivering messages back and forth between his columns. Eventually, all eight fell victim to mechanical failure.

Villa's second card was that from the moment the Americans entered Mexico he had the support, active and passive, of every Mexican. Even the Carrancistas, who were supposedly maintaining law and order, did not want to see Villa captured by Pershing. Information was plentiful for the Americans. Villa had ridden south. He'd ridden north. East. West. He was in Chihuahua City with the señoritas. He'd been wounded. Killed. He'd put horseshoes on backwards so Pershing would

chase off in the wrong direction. He had turned himself into a cactus so that he could observe Pershing at close range.

One rumor turned out to be true. Villa was indeed wounded and incapacitated for a time in late March, when a bullet shattered his shinbone. The shot, however, did not come from an American rifle; it came while Villistas were successfully routing a Carrancista garrison at Guerrero.

The day after the wounded Villa left Guerrero in a carriage, the American Seventh Cavalry, nearly seven hundred strong under Colonel George Dodd, fell upon the celebrating Villistas and inflicted a stinging defeat. That was as close as the U.S. Army would ever get to capturing Villa.

The high point of the American expedition came in May, when Colonel Candelario Cervantes, identified by Pershing as "next to Villa himself, the most able and the most desperate of Villa's band," was killed. A dozen American soldiers were out looking for lost cattle when they were set upon by about twenty Villistas. In the gun battle one trooper was killed, and two Mexicans died. One of the two turned out to be Cervantes.

## The Brink of War

Small victories could not enhance the Americans' popularity. Mexicans continued to detest the U.S. invaders and aided Villa whenever possible. In April a contingent of U.S. soldiers under Major Frank Tomkins—the man who had led the chase for Villa across the border from the Columbus raid—penetrated to Parral, a town 410 miles south of the Texas border. The townspeople spontaneously rose against the soldiers, who retreated in good order. Then more than two hundred Carrancista soldiers joined in, and Tomkins's men had a running fight on their hands until they reached safety. Two Americans were killed and six wounded, including Tomkins, who was winged in the shoulder. Pershing regarded the Mexican attack as unprovoked.

The incident at Parral brought calls from some segments in the United States for a full-scale invasion of Mexico. However, the chief result was that greater restrictions were placed on Pershing, including an order from Funston that he pull back to San Antonio and operate from there. Under pressure from his own people, Carranza announced that Villa

### A Healthy Villa

*As time passed without the punitive expedition's running Villa to earth, the Kansas City Journal grew sarcastic:*

"Since General Pershing was sent out to capture him, Villa has been mortally wounded in the leg and died in a lonely cave. He was assassinated by one of his own band and his grave was identified by a Carranza follower who hoped for a suitable reward from President Wilson. Villa was likewise killed in a brawl at a ranch house where he was engaged in the gentle diversion of burning men and women at the stake. He was also shot on a wild ride and his body cremated. Yet through all these experiences which, it must be confessed, would have impaired the health of any ordinary man, Villa has not only retained the vital spark of life but has renewed his youth and strength. He seems all the better for his vacation, strenuous though it must have been."

*Pershing inspects the U.S. camp in Mexico. Pershing and his troops became frustrated when capturing Villa proved far more difficult than expected.*

was no longer dangerous. He sent General Obregón, whom he had just appointed his secretary of war, to a meeting with generals Funston and Scott at Ciudad Juárez. Obregón formally demanded the removal of U.S. troops from Mexican soil and refused to discuss anything else. Finally, in a marathon meeting, Scott got Obregón to sign an agreement that promised an American withdrawal, but with no date specified, in exchange for stronger efforts on behalf of the Mexican government to wipe out Villa and his followers. It was all so much wasted energy because Carranza refused to sign the document until a specific date for the American withdrawal had been entered.

The hot Mexican summer arrived. American soldiers had begun their expedition as something of a lark. By now they were succumbing to the endless hours of riding and searching the horizon for some sign of Villa, of dust and sweat and conserving water, of living in a country where everyone hated them and a man with a rifle might be lurking around every bend.

In early June the Carrancista comman-der in Chihuahua sent Pershing a message that he had been ordered to oppose any further advances by the American invaders. He told Pershing that he could no longer move east, west, or south—only north. Pershing replied tartly that he had received no such orders from his superiors. When he heard a rumor that Carrancista forces were gathering for an attack sixty miles to the east at a village called Carrizal, eighty-five miles south of Ciudad Juárez, Pershing ordered a reconnaissance. He sent forty-one men of Troop C of the Negro Tenth Cavalry under the command of a white officer, Captain Charles T. Boyd.

Boyd was an unfortunate choice. He was brave but headstrong when the situation called for tact and caution. As he neared Carrizal, Boyd met up with Captain Lewis S. Morey, who was in command of the forty-three men of Troop K of the same regiment. Boyd outranked Morey; he told him that on the next day, he would take all eighty-four troopers into Carrizal and investigate the situation firsthand. Morey objected, but in vain.

The next morning upon reaching Carrizal, Boyd asked the Carrancista commander, General Felix U. Gómez, for permission to ride through the town. Permission was refused. Boyd then ordered his eighty-four men to advance on foot against Gomez's four hundred firmly entrenched troops. The result, predictably, was a slaughter. Twelve Americans died, including Boyd, and twenty-three were captured.

The incident brought the United States and Mexico to the brink of full-scale war. Washington demanded the release of its soldiers. Units of the National Guard were sent to the border, and the bridges crossing the border were seized in anticipation of a full-scale invasion. An army of 150,000 U.S. troops lined the border. Angry editorials and patriotic cartoons proliferated in newspapers in both countries.

Once more, common sense prevailed. On June 28 Carranza, faced with a war he was unlikely to win, ordered all U.S. prisoners released. The two sides agreed to set up a six-man commission—three from the United States, three from Mexico—to decide when the punitive expedition might be withdrawn without too much loss of face to either side. The commission sat for six months but never reached a decision.

The need became less pressing. After Carrizal the expedition took part in no more actions. For six months the Americans kept their patrols restricted to within 150 miles of their Mexican base at Casa Grande, about a hundred miles south of Columbus. All they needed was a good excuse to leave.

## Breaking the Law

*The acquisition of trucks from the punitive expedition was actually illegal, according to Clendenen, in* Blood on the Border. *Frustrated with Washington red tape, General Scott sent for the quartermaster general, Brigadier General Henry G. Sharpe.*

"He asked Sharpe if there were enough trucks to supply Pershing's force. . . . The reply was 'No.' Scott then asked about the cost of a sufficient number of trucks. Sharpe replied, 'About four hundred and fifty thousand dollars.' 'All right,' said Scott, 'send right out and buy those trucks with the necessary traveling garages and mechanics; put a chauffeur on every truck and send them by express to Columbus. . . .' As soon as Secretary [of War] Baker appeared, Scott confessed that he had just committed a serious crime—one for which a penitentiary sentence was prescribed by law. He had spent government funds without an appropriation by Congress. Baker's reply was brief and to the point: 'If anybody goes to jail, I'll be the man.'"

By fall the *New York Herald* could say:

Through no fault of his own, Pershing's Punitive Expedition has become as much a farce from the American standpoint as it is an eyesore to the Mexican people. . . . Each day adds to the burden of its cost . . . and to the ignominy [disgrace] of its position. General Pershing and his command should be recalled without further delay.[45]

## Villa Returns

Meanwhile, Villa had once more resurrected his army. In facing down the United States, he had become a hero to every Mexican, even his enemies. With Pershing and the U.S. Army no longer seriously chasing him, he was able to turn his attention to Carranza. He told his men, "Victory will crown our efforts because justice triumphs in the end. But if death is our destiny, we will fall with our faces to the sky."

In a series of small battles Villa was able to take one Carranza stronghold after another. By October he again controlled much of northern Mexico, and Pershing was asking the War Department for permission to go after him. Permission was never granted; the War Department desperately wanted to go in the opposite direction.

Villa did not try to hold the cities he captured. He preferred hit-and-run tactics. After taking a town, he would extort a "loan" of guns, horses, supplies, and money, shoot a few Carrancistas, and after a few days gallop off again. Because he did

not actually have troops stationed at the areas he controlled, Washington could decide that he did not really control them, and he had become to them simply a roving bandit. Therefore, the United States could pronounce the punitive expedition a success.

Pershing, the dutiful soldier, publicly declared his mission victorious:

Villa has lost most of his prestige and is today little above the ordinary outlaw. The actual capture of Villa would accomplish little or nothing. The problem of Mexico lies a great deal deeper than that. Even [if] Villa were captured, someone else would rise up and take his place. The successful out-

*For eleven months U.S. troops failed to capture, or even catch sight of, the elusive Villa (right).*

law has always appealed to the mind of the Mexican and always will.[46]

But in a private letter written to his father-in-law, Pershing confided:

Dear Francis, it begins to look as though we are to withdraw soon, having been outwitted or outbluffed at every turn of the proceedings. When the true history of this expedition is written, it will not be a very inspiring chapter for school children or even grown-ups to contemplate. Having dashed into Mexico with the intention of eating the Mexicans raw, we turn back at the very first repulse like a whipped cur with his tail between his legs. I would not dare to write this to anybody but you.[47]

On February 5, 1917, after eleven months in Mexico, Pershing and his troops returned to their starting place—Columbus, New Mexico. They had not only failed to capture Pancho Villa, they had not even caught sight of him. The cost of the expedition to the American taxpayer was $130 million.

Most historians regard the punitive expedition as an expensive failure. As for its goal of capturing or killing Villa, it certainly was. On the other hand, the United States did derive some benefits. For one thing, Washington learned just how poorly prepared American forces were to fight a modern, mechanistic war. Secondly, when the United States was drawn into World War I two months later, and Pershing was put in charge of the American Expeditionary Force, the army that he took to Europe possessed a core of veteran troops seasoned in Mexico. If the lessons learned in Mexico were expensive, they were invaluable in France.

# 8 The Slow Peace

With Pershing out of Mexico, relations between that country and the United States could return to normal. However, there was one more twist.

The United States steadfastly refused to be drawn into the war in Europe, even when Germany turned to unrestricted submarine warfare and began sinking American merchant ships that were taking supplies to England and France. Nevertheless, hoping to tie up the United States on its side of the Atlantic, Arthur Zimmerman, the German foreign secretary, put forth an outlandish proposal to the Carranza government: Mexico should declare war on the United States! For its efforts, Mexico would receive generous financial support from Germany and when victory was accomplished would be rewarded with the recovery of its lost territory in Texas, New Mexico, and Arizona. Zimmerman cabled the scheme to the German ambassador in Mexico City in January 1917.

What the Germans did not know was that the British had broken Germany's top code. The explosive contents of the Zimmerman telegram were leaked to the Americans, and the subsequent furor blew the United States into World War I on the side of the Allies.

Carranza denied any knowledge of the German proposal. That was a little hard to believe, but it was unlikely that he could have been tempted into such a harebrained adventure. Whether the punitive expedition was considered a success or a failure, it had demonstrated to Mexico the ability of the U.S. Army to move more or less at will wherever it cared to in Mexico.

## The Constitution of 1917

Pancho Villa's frustration of Pershing's expedition had increased his stature as a romantic hero in Mexico, but Carranza's truculent, or belligerent, insistence on Mexican sovereignty and defiance of its powerful northern neighbor had also improved the first chief's stock. The crusty Carranza was never popular, but his stand against the United States made him tolerable—at least for a while.

In September 1916 Carranza ordered a convention that would consider what changes in the Mexican constitution the revolution had made necessary. It is likely that he envisioned a few cosmetic touches. But the delegates, given their chance, chose to institute sweeping changes and produced what historian Frank Tannenbaum called "the most important event in the history of the Revolution": the constitution of 1917.[48] Wrote historian Morris Weeks Jr.:

> Three articles in particular had national repercussions. Article 3 outlawed private schools and made primary education compulsory. That enraged the Church. Article 123 empowered the government to take over private land or resources for the "general good." That upset big landowners and foreign companies engaged in mining and oil extraction. Article 123 guaranteed many rights for labor, including an eight-hour day, a minimum wage, and the right to strike. That enraged just about everybody—except, of course, labor.[49]

*Fearing the political consequences if he withheld support, Carranza reluctantly signed the 1917 constitution.*

In Mexico City there is a street named Article 123.

These provisions went far beyond anything Carranza had anticipated or wanted, but having initiated the convention, he had little choice but to endorse its wishes. Furthermore, the changes were favored by Alvaro Obregón, and Carranza believed with good cause that Obregón, with his military ability, could overthrow him any time he wished. So regardless of his personal preferences, Carranza signed the constitution into law.

"In sum," wrote Weeks,

> the 1917 constitution gave meaning and purpose to a previously aimless revolution. Not all its articles would be strictly enforced—Mexican politicians knew how to avoid that if necessary—but there they were in black and white, and if Mexico was to move ahead they *had* to mean pretty much what they said.[50]

## Zapata Is Betrayed

Carranza was elected president in 1917, largely as a reward for the constitution. But the revolution had not ended; important events were still to come, but no full-scale battles. The country drifted toward a slow peace with occasional violent interruptions.

Zapata in the south and Villa in the north continued to plague and embarrass Carranza. Zapata was particularly vexing in that his area of operation was so close to Mexico City. The first chief finally sent General Pablo González into the state of Morelos with orders to destroy what he

*Zapata (seated, center) fought back with a vengeance against Carranza's scorched-earth policy. The policy called for the elimination of all Zapatistas and anyone suspected of being sympathetic to them.*

called "the Zapata rabble." González began a scorched-earth policy, systematically wiping out any Zapatistas, any suspected Zapatistas, or anyone believed to be sympathetic to the Zapatistas. He burned whole villages, destroyed crops, herded women and children into detention camps, and hanged every man he could find.

Zapata fought back with craft, heroism, and unspeakable cruelties. One of his favorite methods for executing Carrancistas was to tie them over a fast-growing maguey cactus. The plant would grow a foot or more overnight, slowly impaling the poor victim. The misery for all in Morelos wore on into 1919.

In April 1919 one of González's officers, Colonel Jesus Guajardo, sent word to Zapata that he wished to desert the Carrancistas, taking along his eight hundred troops and a large supply of equipment.

Zapata would never have lived so long without showing extreme caution; he was suspicious of Guajardo's convenient offer. He ordered the colonel to prove himself by capturing the government-held town of Jonacatepec. Obligingly, Guajardo attacked and took the town, completely surprising the Carrancista garrison. Then the colonel shot all the prisoners.

Convinced of Guajardo's intentions, Zapata agreed to meet with him at the hacienda of San Juan Chinameca. Accompanied by ten of his lieutenants, Zapata rode through the gate as bugles blared. Guajardo's soldiers were lined up at attention. The order, "Present arms!" was given. The soldiers raised their rifles and fired, killing Zapata and his companions. For his treachery, Guajardo was promoted to brigadier general and given a reward of twenty-five thousand dollars.

For years afterward many natives of Morelos refused to believe that Zapata was dead. Rumors abounded that on clear nights he could be seen riding over the hills on an elegant white horse.

## The End for Carranza

With Pershing removed as an obstacle, Villa raided in the north with impunity. He found a new way to raise money—by kidnapping Americans and holding them hostage until their families or companies paid the ransom. In October 1918 he grabbed Frank Knotts, the owner of the Erupcion Mining Company and demanded twenty thousand dollars. Knotts's brother brought the money to Villa, but when he looked at the bills, he decided he hated the faces of the gringos on them and demanded that the ransom be paid in gold.

When he raided the mining camp of Cusihuiriachic, he stole ten thousand dollars and burned the entire supply of wood. This, he explained, would force the company to buy more wood and, therefore, provide work for the Mexican people.

By the spring of 1919 Villa had rebuilt his army to about twelve hundred men and replenished his coffers to the point where he could buy all the rifles and ammunition he wanted. At that point he attacked Ciudad Juárez, which was once again in Carrancista hands. The attack came at night. At first all went well, and the federal troops were driven back; but at dawn they counterattacked and regained some ground. When the Villistas returned to the attack, some shots went across the border into El Paso, killing one American soldier and wounding two. Several American civilians were also injured.

That was too much for Brigadier General James B. Erwin, who now commanded the U.S. troops in El Paso. The Carrancistas were warned to get out of the way. Erwin sent two columns of the Sev-

### Loyal to Whom

*Many U.S. leaders opposed entry into war. One reason was that no one knew how the general population might react. According to historian Kennedy:*

"The 1910 census revealed that one out of every three Americans was either foreign-born or the child of a foreign-born parent. Of those 32 million Americans with strong foreign ties, some 10 million came from what were now the enemy countries of Germany and Austria Hungary. Neither their loyalty to the American cause nor even the enthusiasm for the war of millions of other Americans could be taken for granted."

## The Plight of the Mormons

*Villa was particularly hard on Mormon colonists in Chihuahua. Ronald Atkin quotes Anthony W. Ivins, a Mormon elder, in* Revolution! Mexico 1910–1920.

"Most people feel the pincers of the tax collector once a year but the Mormon colonists in Chihuahua not only pay the federal government the regular tax, but hand over any available surplus to Villa and his band of expert and lawless collectors now and then. When Villa needs more money he swoops down on the defenceless colonists and takes it. If the money is not forthcoming he kidnaps some wealthy and influential citizen and holds him for ransom. If the amount is not secured in time, he kills the citizen by way of warning for the future."

enth Cavalry and a brigade of African-American infantry across the bridge. Leading the Seventh Cavalry was Colonel S.R.H. "Tommy" Tomkins, the brother of Frank Tomkins. In a short, sharp, and decisive battle, the Villistas were "scattered like quail," in Tomkins's words.

Once more Villa had been frustrated by the Americans. His army was broken, this time beyond repair. Over the next several months Carrancistas tracked down and executed many Villistas, including Villa's second in command, Felipe Angeles. Shortly thereafter Villa blew up the engine of a train northbound from Chihuahua. Two railway guards were hauled before Villa, who promptly shot them both dead. Then he ordered all the passengers lined up for execution. But just as he was ready to give the command, Villa changed his mind. "Since the execution of my friend Felipe Angeles," he told them, "I have been thirsting for vengeance. That is why I blew up the train. Well, I have

avenged his murder. Now, in memory of him I spare your lives. You may go."[51]

Villa's raids were no longer Carranza's major problem. In the years 1917 to 1919 the Mexican economy was in tatters, industry came to a halt, and inflation was rampant. Disease, including a worldwide influenza epidemic, swept the country. The death rate during the Carranza regime was almost three times that of European countries. Schools were closed for lack of funds. People starved on the streets of Mexico City. Despite the promise of the constitution of 1917, the nation was sliding rapidly toward the abyss.

Under Carranza's auspices government corruption reached new highs, exacerbating all the other troubles. What Carranza really wanted in a government was a repeat of the Díaz regime, with himself replacing Díaz. He did not, however, have Díaz's knack for bypassing the constitution and gaining reelection. As the presidential election of 1920 approached, it became obvious that only one man had both the ability and the widespread support to lead the troubled country out of the morass—Alvaro Obregón. That did not keep Carranza from putting forth his own handpicked candidate, a nonentity who everyone agreed would have made a fine bookkeeper. In the meantime, General Pablo González, who had confidently expected to receive Carranza's backing, announced his own candidacy. All three candidates campaigned for the presidency, but the election never took place.

Early in 1920 yet another rebellion blew up in Sonora, led by the state's governor, Adolfo de la Huerta. At the same time, Carranza tried to weaken Obregón by using the treason trial of another officer to discredit him. The attempt backfired, and Carranza found even his oldest hangers-on drifting away. Obregón and another general, Plutarco Elías Calles, moved on the capital. Carranza decided to flee once more to Veracruz, taking five million pesos in gold and silver from the national treasury with him. He never made it. On the way he left the train with one of his remaining generals. The next day his body was found in an Indian hut. The general said that Carranza had committed suicide. If so, it was by the rather unusual method of shooting himself in the chest three times.

## Villa Retires

The Sonora governor, Adolfo de la Huerta, was chosen interim president by the Mexican legislature and held office for six months. Frank and honest, he worked hard at healing his country's wounds during his presidency, and to a great extent succeeded. He announced that all Mexicans in exile for their political activities were free to return. His most spectacular achievement was to negotiate the retirement of Pancho Villa. Although Obregón and Calles both opposed any dealing with Villa, de la Huerta was able to convince the old bandit to leave off his raids and accept a twenty-five-thousand-acre hacienda in the state of Durango just across the border from Parral in Villa's home state of Chihuahua. He retained fifty bodyguards paid by the state. The rest of his men were given a year's wages and parcels of land.

After retiring to his hacienda, Pancho

*Adolfo de la Huerta served six productive months as Mexico's interim president. His most notable accomplishment was successfully negotiating a deal for Villa's retirement.*

## How the Money Goes

*The English newspaper* Daily Mail *printed an article by "An Englishman Just Returned from Mexico." It said in part:*

"The Mexican government has been increasing old taxes and inventing new ones ruthlessly; enormous sums have flowed into the government exchequer [treasury]. . . . Yet despite this colossal taxation the public services are shamefully neglected. For instance, public education is at a standstill. There are no funds to pay the professors and teachers. How the money goes is proved by the fact that half a dozen or more men have become millionaires . . . from nothing within the last five years. One of them is a relation of Carranza."

Villa lived comfortably for several years. But old hatreds die hard. Relatives of some whom Villa had harmed during the revolution raised a "kill Villa" fund of ten thousand dollars.

On July 19, 1923, Villa and five bodyguards drove into Parral in his Dodge automobile to witness the christening of the child of one of his men. They spent the night at the hotel and set off the next morning to return to the hacienda. Villa was at the wheel.

As they slowed at a corner, a pumpkin seed seller called out, "Viva Villa!" The cheer was a signal to the assassins waiting around the corner. Villa raised his arm to acknowledge the cheer just as a fusillade of shots rang out. He was killed instantly, seven shots striking him, though legend has him struggling out of the wrecked auto and killing one of his assassins before he died. Only one of the bodyguards lived, and he was badly wounded. The Dodge had more than forty bullet holes.

In the aftermath one of the assassins was arrested, but he served only six months before he was released and made a colonel in the army. On his deathbed in 1951 he insisted, "I'm not a murderer. I rid humanity of a monster."[52]

Many claimed that Obregón was behind the assassination, but no evidence has ever been uncovered to link him to the event. On the other hand, his leniency in dealing with the lone convicted assassin would indicate that he was not particularly heartbroken to learn of Villa's death.

Although he had previously prepared an elaborate mausoleum, or tomb, in Chihuahua City, Villa was buried in a simple grave in Parral. Then, in perhaps the most bizarre twist of all, his grave was broken into in 1926 and his head was stolen. It has never been recovered.

# Why Villa?

From Francisco Madero, who died in 1913, until Alvaro Obregón, who was elected in 1920, Mexico had ten presidents, counting the various interim and provisional varieties. A few, such as Victoriano Huerta and Venustiano Carranza, left their marks for better or for worse. Certainly Adolfo de la Huerta benefited his country. Most of the others had reigns of short duration and little consequence. One lasted a record forty-six minutes.

Obregón proved to be the best of the lot. A sturdy realist, he became the first president since Díaz to serve a full term in office. In land reform he distributed seven times as many acres as Carranza but was careful not to go so far as to disrupt Mexico's frail economy. Labor made strides under Obregón as Article 123 became more than just words on paper. His greatest achievement came in education. Money that had once been siphoned into politicians' pockets was at last used to build the nation. Normal, or teacher-training, schools were created, and hundreds of teachers were trained and sent to the most remote parts of the country.

Although the worst of the revolution

*Although he was an effective president and made important strides in implementing constitutional reform, Alvaro Obregón could not completely quell the flames of revolution in Mexico.*

*Whether he is judged a hero or a monster, Pancho Villa deserves credit for helping to achieve greater citizen rights and reform in a country riddled with corruption.*

was past, even Obregón could not bring complete peace to this troubled country. Toward the end of his term a reluctant de la Huerta led a small, unsuccessful rebellion against him. In 1928, after Calles had served a term as president, Obregón ran again and was elected. But before he could serve, he was assassinated by a fanatic. Occasional spates of violence continue in Mexico even to this day. A candidate for president was murdered in 1994, and a rebellion among the Chiapas Indians of the south was led by a young man who acknowledged he had studied the tactics of Zapata and Villa.

Of the leaders who crossed the bloody stage that was Mexico in the years between 1910 and 1920, Alvaro Obregón was surely the most competent when both military and political achievements are considered. Venustiano Carranza was perhaps the most opportunistic, although some might argue for Victoriano Huerta. Francisco Madero was no doubt the most idealistic, followed closely by Emiliano Zapata. Yet, it is the fascinating, volatile Pancho Villa whose name was best known at the time and is still remembered today.

Villa, with his scruffy clothes, wide grin, unpredictable rages, vainglorious, or boastful, pronouncements, and undeniable courage, is the very personification of the outlaw-patriot so often depicted in song and legend. As such, he is much more a living person to today's reader than many of the other revolutionary figures. Indeed, we can only believe that in his day Villa was more real to the average Mexican than others who from time to time held more political power. And that explains why he always found men who would follow him and, when necessary, die for him.

Although Villa spent ten years fighting for Mexico's freedom, the central event of his life was his raid on Columbus and the resulting punitive expedition, which he frustrated so completely. Other battles won and lost were of more importance in the ultimate outcome of the revolution, but it is the Columbus raid and its aftermath that captures the imagination.

To most Americans and some Mexicans, Villa was indeed a monster. Or at the very best, a gangster. Cruel, vindictive, and unpredictable, he was certainly a mass murderer even under the loose definitions applied during revolutions. Did the gains made by Mexican citizens after 1920—gains Villa was in part responsible for causing—justify the amount of blood on his hands? Or, to put it another way, given his country's dark history, could anyone except Villa begin with so little and help bring so much change?

To many Mexicans Villa is a hero—a Robin Hood on horseback who rose from abject poverty to defy and, in effect, defeat the colossus, or giant, of the north. In a country that too often has bowed to the wishes and whims of its powerful northern neighbor, he became a symbol of Mexican pride and an example of the power of a single individual to triumph against the odds.

# Notes

### Chapter 1: "Viva Villa! Viva México!"

1. Quoted in Ronald Atkin, *Revolution! Mexico 1910–1920.* New York: John Day, 1969.
2. Quoted in Atkin, *Revolution.*
3. Quoted in Atkin, *Revolution.*
4. Quoted in Atkin, *Revolution.*
5. Paul Espinosa, "The Hunt for Pancho Villa." Narrated by Linda Hunt. Boston: WGBH Educational Foundation and Galan Productions, 1993.
6. Espinosa, "The Hunt for Pancho Villa."
7. *The New York Times,* March 10, 1916.
8. Quoted in Atkin, *Revolution.*
9. Espinosa, "The Hunt for Pancho Villa."
10. *The New York Times,* March 11, 1916.
11. *The New York Times,* March 11, 1916.

### Chapter 2: Heritage of Blood

12. Atkin, *Revolution.*
13. Quoted in Jessie Peterson and Thelma Cox Knoles, eds., *Pancho Villa: Intimate Recollections by People Who Knew Him.* New York: Hastings House, 1977.
14. Quoted in Atkin, *Revolution.*
15. Atkin, *Revolution.*

### Chapter 3: A False Dawn

16. Quoted in Peterson and Knoles, *Pancho Villa.*
17. Quoted in Peterson and Knoles, *Pancho Villa.*
18. Quoted in Peterson and Knoles, *Pancho Villa.*
19. Quoted in Peterson and Knoles, *Pancho Villa.*
20. Charles Macomb Flandrau, *Viva Mexico.* New York: Appleton, 1908.

21. Peterson and Knoles, *Pancho Villa.*
22. E. J. Dillon, *Mexico on the Verge.* New York: Hutchinson, 1922. Quoted in Atkin, *Revolution.*
23. Frank Tannenbaum, *Peace by Revolution.* New York: Columbia University Press, 1931.
24. Quoted in Atkin, *Revolution.*
25. John Kenneth Turner, *Barbarous Mexico.* New York: Cassell, 1911.

### Chapter 4: Another Turn in the Wind

26. Quoted in Leone B. Moats, *Thundered in Their Veins.* London: 1933.
27. Quoted in Atkin, *Revolution.*
28. Quoted in Atkin, *Revolution.*
29. Quoted in Atkin, *Revolution.*

### Chapter 5: The Allies Fall Out

30. Quoted in Atkin, *Revolution.*
31. Quoted in Espinosa, "The Hunt for Pancho Villa."
32. Quoted in Espinosa, "The Hunt for Pancho Villa."
33. Quoted in Espinosa, "The Hunt for Pancho Villa."
34. Quoted in Espinosa, "The Hunt for Pancho Villa."
35. Quoted in Martin Luis Guzman, *Memoirs of Pancho Villa.* Austin: University of Texas Press, 1965.

### Chapter 6: Betrayed

36. Quoted in Espinosa, "The Hunt for Pancho Villa."
37. Quoted in Espinosa, "The Hunt for Pancho Villa."
38. Quoted in Atkin, *Revolution.*
39. Quoted in H. Hamilton Fyfe, *The Real Mexico.* New York: Heinemann, 1914.

## Chapter 7: General Pershing Invades

40. Quoted in Leon Wolfe, "Black Jack's Mexican Goose Chase," *American Heritage*, June 1962.

41. Quoted in Espinosa, "The Hunt for Pancho Villa."

42. Quoted in Wolfe, "Black Jack's Mexican Goose Chase."

43. Wolfe, "Black Jack's Mexican Goose Chase."

44. Wolfe, "Black Jack's Mexican Goose Chase."

45. Quoted in Atkin, *Revolution*.

46. Quoted in Espinosa, "The Hunt for Pancho Villa."

47. Quoted in Espinosa, "The Hunt for Pancho Villa."

## Chapter 8: The Slow Peace

48. Tannenbaum, *Peace by Revolution*.

49. Morris Weeks Jr., *Hello Mexico*. New York: W. W. Norton, 1970.

50. Weeks, *Hello Mexico*.

51. Quoted by Dillon, in Atkin, *Revolution*.

52. Quoted by *Time*, June 4, 1951, in Atkin, *Revolution*.

# For Further Reading

Compiled with the aid of Sue Foster, District Young Adult/Outreach Specialist, the Carnegie Library of Pittsburgh, Pennsylvania.

### Pancho Villa Biographies

Oren Arnold, *Pancho Villa: Mexican Centaur*. Tuskaloosa, AL: Portals Press, 1979. Focuses on Villa's military exploits.

Carol Gaskin and Guthridge Gaskin, *Death Mask of Pancho Villa*. New York: Bantam, 1987. Part of the Time Machine series.

Martin Luis Guzman, *The Eagle and the Serpent*. Translated from the Spanish by Harriet de Onis. Gloucester, MA: P. Smith, 1969. The author was a participant in the revolution during the Madero-Carranza years.

Larry A. Harris, *Pancho Villa: Strong Man of the Revolution*. Silver City, NM: High-Lonesome Books, 1949. A basic biography viewing Villa as hero.

Steven O'Brien, *Pancho Villa: Mexican Revolutionary*. New York: Chelsea House, 1994. Part of the Hispanics of Achievement series, aimed at grades six through twelve.

Jessie Peterson and Thelma Cox Knoles, eds., *Pancho Villa: Intimate Recollections by People Who Knew Him*. New York: Hastings House, 1977. Accounts from some who admired him and others who hated him.

Edgcumb Pinchon, *Viva Villa: A Recovery of the Real Pancho Villa, Peon, Bandit, Soldier, Patriot*. New York: Ayer, 1933. An admiring biography.

Jim Tuck, *Pancho Villa and John Reed: Two Faces of Romantic Revolution*. Tucson: University of Arizona Press, 1984. John Reed was an American communist who eventually died in the Soviet Union.

### The Mexican Revolution

David G. LaFrance, *The Mexican Revolution in Puebla, 1908–1913*. Wilmington, DE: Scholarly Resources, 1989. Focuses on the origins and results of the early revolution in the state of Puebla rather than on the nationwide scene.

Herbert Molloy Mason Jr., *The Great Pursuit*. New York: Random House, 1970. The story of Pershing's punitive expedition of 1916–1917.

John David Ragan, *Emiliano Zapata*. New York: Chelsea House, 1989. Part of the Hispanics of Achievement series, aimed at grades six through twelve.

Rebecca Stefoff, *Independence and Revolution in Mexico, 1810–1940*. New York: Facts On File, 1993. Views the 1910–1920 revolution in the context of the entire Mexican revolutionary movement.

R. Conrad Stein, *The Mexican Revolution, 1910–1920*. New York: Macmillan, 1994. More tightly focused than the Stefoff book. Contains material on Villa, Madero, Obregón, Zapata, and the other heroes and villains.

# Works Consulted

Ronald Atkin, *Revolution! Mexico 1910–1920*. New York: John Day, 1969. Excellent and readable account of the revolutionary period, written with clarity and an eye for anecdote.

Clarence C. Clendenen, *Blood on the Border: The United States Army and the Mexican Irregulars*. London: Macmillan, 1969. Detailed account of the happenings along the border, as seen primarily from the view of the U.S. Army.

Charles C. Cumberland, *Mexico: The Struggle for Modernity*. New York: Oxford University Press, 1968. Emphasizes changes in Mexico's economic and social systems.

Paul Espinosa, "The Hunt for Pancho Villa." Narrated by Linda Hunt. Boston: WGBH Educational Foundation and Galan Productions, 1993. This fine one-hour video, shown as part of *The American Experience* on the Public Broadcasting System, combines motion pictures and still photography from the period with interviews with historians and survivors of Villa's raids and Pershing's punitive expedition.

Charles Macomb Flandrau, *Viva Mexico*. New York: Appleton, 1908. Written toward the end of the Díaz regime, this makes for an interesting comparison with later opinions.

Paul Horgan, *Great River: The Rio Grande in North American History*, vol. 2: *Mexico and the United States*. New York: Rinehart, 1954. Detailed history of the Rio Grande region.

William Weber Johnson, and the editors of *Life*, *Mexico*. Part of the *Life World Library Series*. New York: Time, Inc., 1961. Like other books in this series, briefly but authoritatively traces the entire history of Mexico from ancient times to today. Excellent charts and illustrations.

Clarke Newlon, *The Men Who Made Mexico*. New York: Dodd, Mead, 1973. The story of Mexico told through the lives of its leaders, heroes, and villains from the time of the Aztecs to recently. Díaz, Madero, Carranza, Obregón, Zapata, and Villa are all profiled.

*The New York Times*, March 10, 1916, 1:5, and March 11, 1916, 10:1. Villa's raid is the main story in the March 10 edition, with a wealth of details. The follow-up editorial the next day mirrors most Americans' reactions.

Morris Weeks Jr., *Hello Mexico*. New York: W. W. Norton, 1970. A look at Mexico's history, customs, and geography, with a good chapter on the revolution of 1910–1920.

Leon Wolfe, "Black Jack's Mexican Goose Chase," *American Heritage*, June 1962. Excellent article covering the Pershing expedition.

John Womack Jr., *Zapata and the Mexican Revolution*. New York: Alfred A. Knopf, 1969. Focuses on Zapata's role in the southern part of the revolution.

# Index

# Picture Credits

# About the Author

Bob Carroll is the author of more than twenty books and over two hundred articles that are primarily about sports history. His credits include *The Hidden Game of Football* (with John Thorn and Pete Palmer), *Pro Football: When the Grass Was Real, Baseball Between the Lies*, and *The Importance of Napoleon Bonaparte*, Lucent Books. In addition to writing he is a sports artist whose illustrations appear regularly in several national publications. He lives in North Huntingdon, Pennsylvania.

22.59

```
--         Carroll, Bob,
B            1936-
Villa
C          The importance of
             Pancho Villa.
```

| DATE | | | |
|---|---|---|---|
| | | | |
| | | | |
| | | | |
| | | | |
| | | | |
| | | | |
| | | | |
| | | | |
| | | | |
| | | | |
| | | | |
| | | | |
| | | | |
| | | | |

BAKER & TAYLOR